KT-440-098

brilliant

economics

Making sense of the big ideas

Phil Thornton

PEARSON

Harlow, England • London • New York • Boston • San Francisco • Toronto • Sydney • Auckland • Singapore • Hong Kong
Tokyo • Seoul • Taipei • New Delhi • Cape Town • São Paulo • Mexico City • Madrid • Amsterdam • Munich • Paris • Milan

PEARSON EDUCATION LIMIT

Edinburgh Gate
Harlow CM20 2JE
Tel: +44 (0)1279 623623
Fax: +44 (0)1279 431059
Website: www.pearson.com/uk

First published 2013 (print and elec

© Phil Thornton 2013 (print and ele

The right of Phil Thornton to be identified as author of this work has been asserted by him in accordance with the Copyright, Designs and Patents Act 1988.

Pearson Education is not responsible for the content of third-party internet sites.

ISBN: 978-1-292-00303-0 (print)
        978-1-292-00320-7 (PDF)
        978-1-292-00321-4 (ePub)

British Library Cataloguing-in-Publication Data
A catalogue record for the print edition is available from the British Library

Library of Congress Cataloging-in-Publication Data
A catalog record for the print edition is available from the Library of Congress

10 9 8 7 6 5 4 3 2 1
17 16 15 14 13

Print edition typeset in 10/14 Plantin Std by 30
Print edition printed and bound in Great Britain by Henry Ling, at the Dorset Press, Dorchester, Dorset

NOTE THAT ANY PAGE CROSS-REFERENCES REFER TO THE PRINT EDITION

Contents

About the author

Phil Thornton has written about economics, finance and business for 20 years and spent almost a decade at *The Independent* as its economic correspondent. Since 2007 he has run Clarity Economics, a consultancy and freelance writing service he set up after going freelance. Clarity Economics (www.clarityeconomics.com) looks at all areas of business and economics including macroeconomics, world trade, financial markets fiscal policy, and tax and regulation.

In 2010 he won the Feature Journalist of the Year award in the WorkWorld Media Awards. In 2007 he won the title of Print Journalist of the Year in the same awards. He lives in London with his wife and three sons.

Author acknowledgements

I would like to thank my family and friends who have helped and supported me in the writing of this book. Thanks in particular to all of the publishing team at Pearson and especially to Chris Cudmore whose advice and guidance throughout the writing process was invaluable. I would also like to thank Dr Chris Jones of Aston Business School for his advice at the book's early stages.

Publisher acknowledgements

We are grateful to the following for permission to reproduce copyright material:

Figure 1.1 from Office for National Statistics, http://www.ons.gov.uk/ons/infographics/how-ons-statistics-explain-the-uk-economy/index.html, Source: Office for National Statistics licensed under the Open Government Licence v.1.0.; Table 2.1 adapted from *World Development Indicators Database*, World Bank, 18 September 2012, reproduced with permission, http://web.worldbank.org/WBSITE/EXTERNAL/0,contentMDK:22547097~pagePK:50016803~piPK:50016805~theSitePK:13,00.html; Table 2.2 adapted from IMF, *World Economic Outlook*, October 2012, Table 1.1, http://www.imf.org/external/pubs/ft/weo/2012/02/pdf/c1.pdf, reproduced with permission. Figures 6.1 and 6.2 from *Executive Summary, Budget 2012*, http://cdn.hmtreasury.gov.uk/budget2012_executive_summary.pdf, Contains public sector information licensed under the Open Government Licence (OGL) v1.0.http://www.nationalarchives.gov.uk/doc/open-government-licence/open-government.

In some instances we have been unable to trace the owners of copyright material, and we would appreciate any information that would enable us to do so.

Introduction

Economics is one of those subjects that many people are scared to talk about. Like astrophysics it contains unusual words and strange phrases while its practitioners' books and articles contain incomprehensible equations that use Greek letters. But unlike astrophysics people use economics every day – without even knowing it. Anyone who has signed a mortgage deed, taken up a university course or decided how to pay for their shopping has made an economic decision. If they have taken an action based on instinct or because someone they knew did the same thing, then it may turn out to be a worse outcome than if they used even the most basic economic rationales.

Taking out a mortgage involves making some sort of assessment about the interest rate, whether you can make the payments and whether the house is overvalued – and if so, whether you are buying it in order to get nearer a good school. Going to university, especially in the UK or the US, involves deciding that the qualification you will receive will improve your chances of getting a well-paid job that will not only allow you to repay the loan for the tuition fees but will ensure that you earn more over your lifetime. Finally, as you stand at the supermarket checkout you have to decide whether you value having liquid cash in your purse or wallet more than you worry about whether you will be able to pay the credit card bill when it comes in a month's time. Economics, like love in the song by the band Wet Wet Wet, is all around us all of the time. Some of us just don't know it.

⬤ brilliant example

Someone buying a new car can make the decision for many different reasons. The point of this book is to show that by thinking like an economist you will make a better choice. Many may plump for a model that looks trendy or fast or because someone they knew got one. An economist will want to know how fuel-efficient it is and how much maintenance it will need, so they can work out what the 'real' long-term cost is. She will also need to think about the amount of money it will cost her upfront and whether it would be better to buy a cheaper car and use the difference to buy other goods that she would otherwise have to go without. She might also think about whether the car fits with the image she wants to present to colleagues at work or home. Finally, she will estimate how much the car might be worth in a few years' time when she comes to sell it. If you do all those things then you are half way to thinking like an economist. Substitute the word 'motorway' for 'car' to see how governments think about these decisions.

The aim of this book therefore is to take the mystery out of economics. It will introduce you to the real stars of economics – the now dead figures whose innovative thinking changed the way people looked at the world and even gave their surnames to whole economic schools of thought. It will also explain the key concepts of macroeconomics that appear in newspapers, website forums and on television every day. Never has being fluent in the language of economics been more important than now, as the world's economies struggle to escape the aftershocks of the financial crisis that began in 2008 and the more recent European sovereign debt disaster. In the wake of the crash some economists accused their colleagues of developing economic forecasts and doctrines based on theories that had little basis in real life. Perhaps if more people had been more fluent in economics there would have been more warning flags raised as the seeds of the West's financial system were sown.

The book will start with an overview of economics that highlights the division between microeconomics and macroeconomics. From that launch pad we can blast off to visit 11 satellites – key economic concepts that fill our TV screens, front pages and web pages every day. In the first few months of 2013 I made a note of headlines and stories from non-business media that highlighted how important it is to have an implicit knowledge of economics. These stories showed how pervasive economics is in modern life and why it helps us read the runes of our society.

Chapter 1: Economics – the business of life

On 11th February 2013, BBC Radio 4 spoke of 'creative destruction' in their Analysis programme. The global financial crisis and the ensuing recession have propelled the whole world of macroeconomics to the top of everyone's agenda. As businesses have gone bust, people have lost their jobs, and families have struggled to hang on to their homes, the debate over the solutions to the economic problems have become the stuff of debates in the café, pub and living room. Words like Keynesianism, fiscal austerity, real incomes, negative equity, double-dip recession and sovereign default are used in everyday debate in a way that would have seemed jarring just five years ago. Creative destruction is a strange-sounding theory which says that the process of innovation by new businesses that puts old ones out of business is an essential part of the capitalist growth cycle. It is hard to imagine a half-hour programme on prime time BBC radio devoted to one economic theory before 2008.

Chapter 2: The miracle of growth

On 16th January 2013, *The Daily Telegraph* reported that Britain was going to drop out of the world's top 10 economies. Economic growth is the Holy Grail for both macroeconomists and politicians needing to get re-elected. Stable, long-term and sustainable increase in economic activity is the surest way to deliver higher living standards. As many people have seen in recent times, when the economic machine slows it can make them poorer and affect their lives in many different ways. This chapter will look at what makes up economic growth and how it is measured and will also look at the different phases of growth that countries go through as they move from the early, developing stage into the middle income bracket and into the developed economy group. This story is a reminder that countries moving through the development process will post faster growth rates than more mature economies and will ultimately catch up their erstwhile rivals. In this case PricewaterhouseCoopers predicted that Britain would be overtaken by Mexico and Indonesia in the next four decades to push the nation's GDP to 11th place in world rankings. However, on the key measure of GDP per person – how rich the average citizen is – the UK will still rank fourth in 2050.

Chapter 3: Business cycles – from boom to bust and back again

On 19th February 2013, ITV News reported that young people were being put off driving. The idea of a business cycle moving through four phases of recovery, strong growth, overheating and recession is one of the core concepts for economists. While there are many different theories both about its causes and its duration, clearly knowing where you are at any given time is key to making important long-term decisions. In this case the prolonged five-year downturn period of the most recent economic cycle has hurt consumers and businesses across the economy. This recent decline of 20% or 200,000 young drivers deciding not to spend money on a driving test is linked in part to the fact that unemployment has increased sharply, while the incomes after tax of those aged between 16 and 26 are falling faster than those of any other age group.

Chapter 4: Work and wages

On 12th February 2013, the *Evening Standard* reported the words of a young graduate who explained she was not above working in a shop, but just expected to be paid. Having a job is one of most people's primary needs in a modern economy as work gives people income, self-respect and contact with a wider network of connections. But the labour market is one of the most complex parts of the economy and one where the interests of workers, employers and occasionally the government are most likely to collide. Understanding the different explanations for how jobs are created, how wages are set, why unemployment rises and the best way to get people back into work is essential to taking part in political debate. Since the recession of 2008 unemployment has soared on both sides of the Atlantic, and particularly in the over-indebted countries of southern Europe. Governments of all political hues have rolled out measures to bring unemployment down. However, some, such as the scheme in the UK to make some benefit claimants do unpaid work to gain experience, have run into stiff opposition from the people they were intended to help – and in this case from the High Court as well.

Chapter 5: The pain of inflation

On 15th February 2013, the *Evening Standard* reported that beef prices were starting to soar as customer demand for prime cuts hit a new high. Other than unemployment, inflation is one of the economic concepts that affect people most directly and which they are keen to complain about. While most people probably recognise inflation through its impact on their wallet or purse, they may not understand how it is calculated and how it can quickly turn into either hyperinflation or deflation. This news story, which points to a potential spike in prime cuts of beef in the wake of the revelations over the presence of horsemeat in processed food, is an example of how changes in demand and supply can move prices. The same reaction took place when it was reported that a meteorite had hit a Russian zinc plant, briefly pushing up the price of the metal. The chapter looks at the definition of inflation, how it is measured, and why and how economic policymakers try to keep it low and stable.

Chapter 6: The role of government

On 12th February 2013, *The Daily Telegraph* quoted Andrew Dilnot, the economist put in charge of a review of social costs, as saying that a cap of £75,000 for patients was too high. The financial crisis has put the role of central government back at the centre of economic policy – and into the heart of the debate over how to run an economy. Before the global recession there had been a growing consensus among politicians of both sides of the political divide that the government should not interfere in the running of the economy. Many policymakers have argued that governments only distort the smooth operating of the economic system. But the scale of the recession prompted governments to act by using vast quantities of public money to try to kick-start a recovery. While it succeeded in its aim by averting a depression, it left many countries with large public sector deficits that will take many years and a lot of sacrifices by different groups of taxpayers to return to balance. But raising taxes or cutting spending will always anger someone. In the case of this news story, plans to limit the amount that the elderly in England must pay before the government steps in has caused deep controversy.

Chapter 7: Interest rates, monetary policy and central banks

On 15th February 2013, *The Independent* urged people not to give up the savings habit. Anyone who has a mortgage, or has taken out a loan with their bank to fund their business or pay for a holiday knows that interest rates matter. Equally, anyone who has tucked their nest egg away in a savings account will know that the interest rate is one of the most important parts of the deal. When asked who sets interest rates, an increasingly large number of people will say correctly that it is the central bank. But not many will know why and how they do this. This chapter looks at why central banks set the interest rate and how they decide whether to leave it on hold, raise it or, as has been seen more recently, cut it. But this is not the only interest rate. The costs of borrowing and the rewards of savings are based on interest rates that are driven by factors other than just the official rate. The chapter looks at how those market rates are set and explains the controversy over LIBOR. Record low interest rates in the US, UK, Europe, Japan and elsewhere have made life hard for savers, who, as this story indicates, have to do some hard thinking if they want to receive an income from their savings without taking too much risk.

Chapter 8: Money and finance

On 18th February 2013, the *Daily Mail* reported the claims of the incoming Bank of England governor that the UK could introduce plastic notes. The financial system has been the focus of concern across the world in the wake of the series of financial failures across Europe and America that culminated in the failure of Lehman Brothers bank in the US which triggered the global recession of 2008 and 2009. There is no shortage of headlines about money and finance even five years after the crash. As homes and shares have lost value and jobs have been cut, a growing number of families are forced to count every penny. Just as money is important to households in their everyday life, it is also an essential concept for economists in their struggle to understand how the economy works. Money exists not just as notes and coins but also increasingly in many different forms that are used by both households and businesses. But to understand how they fit together and how the ability to borrow money was a key ingredient in the 2008 financial crisis, this chapter first takes the reader back to ancient history to understand the origins of money. And although that may seem irrelevant now, the news story above shows how even notes and coins are still the centre of financial innovation.

Chapter 9: Housing and property

On 12th February 2013, the *Daily Mail* reported how first-time buyers needed 10 years to raise a deposit. A home is the most expensive thing that anyone will buy and whether one is renting or paying a mortgage that bill will probably make up a large chunk of a household's monthly outgoings. But while a home is a basic necessity of life, it is also an asset that is subject to the laws of supply and demand. This chapter looks at the factors that drive house prices and rents and how house prices in particular can have a major impact on economic stability and are always a major part of any economic downturn. Over the last few decades, house prices have repeatedly seemed to move way out of line with people's incomes. This news story highlights how house prices can be driven by factors outside most people's control and how these factors can make it increasingly hard for new buyers to get a foot on the housing ladder.

Chapter 10: Trade and currencies

On 12th February 2013, the *Daily Mail* reported that China was now the world's largest trading nation. Global trade has dramatically changed the range of goods that most households can buy and has brought their prices down dramatically. But while we take the benefits of these trades for granted, few people understand the complex economic relationships that influence which goods and services countries trade with each other, the prices at which they buy and sell and how this influences – and is influenced by – exchange rates. But among those who have taken the time to study the subject there are some who have become very angry at the inequalities they say that the international trade system brings to certain groups of people and parts of the world. And as the news story above indicates, global trade is raising concerns in the West that emerging markets are somehow stealing their jobs and livelihoods. This chapter unpicks the complex relationships involved in global trade and currencies and looks at the latest thinking on issues such as fair trade and consumers' responsibility to ensure their favourite T-shirt does not come at a cost to overseas workers.

Chapter 11: The future of economics

On 2nd February 2013, *The Observer* reported that the former Foreign Secretary David Miliband was striving to end the lawlessness of the seas. The failure of mainstream economics to predict the financial crisis and, before that, its inability to account for pollution and climate change has fuelled interest in alternative ways of looking at economics, such as fusing it with psychology to produce behavioural economics, or finding ways to ensure that the world does not suffer an environmental catastrophe. This story looks at how moves by former Foreign Secretary David Miliband to stop decades of over-exploitation have caused trillions of pounds' worth of fish catches to be lost. At its heart is the economic idea of the 'tragedy of the commons' that shows how the running down of resources that are largely owned by no one, are exploited by anyone and are poorly unregulated leads to over-fishing.

Hopefully this shows that an understanding of economics will help decipher news stories and public debates that nowadays assume a comprehension of basic economic concepts. While economics may seem like a scarily complicated subject, the truth is that it has become like that because economists prefer it that way. If 'normal' people can't get to grips with the subject matter then they are less able to challenge the professionals. If there is one lesson that the financial crisis has taught us, it 'is' that: it is essential that those making forecasts and policy prescriptions can be held to account.

This book aims to show how the uses of economics at a national and global level can be broken into some key concepts. It seeks to demystify those concepts and show that they are both relatively easy to understand and often relate to ways of thinking that many of us already use. However, it is only an introduction to economics – there will be none of the graphs and equations found in textbooks or treatises. Hopefully it will grab your attention and make you find out about some of its key ideas in more detail. There is an immense treasure trove of writing out there that awaits you. In the meantime, this book should be a map to guide you through the economics that you already encounter every day.

CHAPTER 1

Economics – the business of life

'If all economists were laid end to end, they would still not reach a conclusion.'

George Bernard Shaw, author and playwright, 1856-1950

E conomists have never had a good press. Someone could probably compile a highly amusing – and long – book of jokes about this profession. But beneath many of the jokes are a number of assumptions about what economics is and what economists do. Some of these criticisms have a lot of truth to them but many of them have been overtaken by advances in economic thinking.

To keep the mood light-hearted we can use a series of the best-known jokes to illustrate some of those assumptions. But before doing that it is worth thinking about the recent damage to the reputation of economics inflicted by the financial crisis that began in 2007 – or more accurately by economists' failure to predict it.

In late 2008, about a month after the collapse of Lehman Brothers investment bank triggered a global downturn, Her Majesty the Queen was visiting the London School of Economics to open a new £71 million building. She asked the attendant economists: 'Why did no-one see this coming?' Headlines flashed around the world as it struck a chord with the millions of people directly affected by the recession. Only a handful of economists predicted the ensuing credit crunch. In the wake of the crash, economists such as Nobel laureate Joseph Stiglitz said the failure was due to the fact that the models used by mainstream economists did not account for the wild swings in credit markets that took place in 2008 and were too heavily based on the idea that markets would correct themselves.

Whatever the criticisms, there is no doubt that the scale of the credit crunch, the global recession and the eurozone debt crisis have put economics back on the top of the political agenda and at the centre of dinner party conversations across the world. The debate about the causes of the recession and the best medicine for growth will continue for years and economic theory and practice will be a vital element of that. It also means there has never been a better time to look at the evolution of economics as a discipline. But first, some jokes...

How many economists does it take...?

Q: How many economists does it take to change a light bulb? A: Two. One to assume the existence of a ladder and one to change the bulb

One criticism of economics is that it relies on models and assumptions that assume patterns of behaviour which are not always found in real life. But economics is a science rather than an art and so seeks to draw up laws and theories through a scientific process. Just as a physical scientist would set up a laboratory experiment to test the interaction of two chemicals, so economists try to run models to test a theory.

Q: How many economists does it take to change a light bulb? A: It depends on the wage rate

Non-economists often think that economists are only concerned with money. This may be due to the fact that so many economists in the public eye work for investment banks or other financial institutions and so are seen as speaking on behalf of organisations whose motivation is making money. It may also be the focus of economics on efficiency that gives the impression it is only interested in money. In fact economics seeks to maximise the 'welfare' of an individual or of society, which increasingly includes concepts such as environmental welfare.

Q: How many economists does it take to change a light bulb? A: None. If the light bulb needed changing the market would have already done it

One assumption that is at the heart of economics – and particularly the neoclassical doctrine, as we shall see shortly – is the idea of the rational agents. This comes close to the criticism of the economists' profession in the run-up to the crash. If all people in an economy act in their own best interests all of the time then if part of the economy, such as, say, house or share prices, appear to move out of line, the collective impact of the transactions of rational agents will bring that back to a long-term sustainable level. However, economics is increasingly moving to embrace other disciplines such as psychology to help understand how people do behave.

> economics is 'the ordinary business of life'

The birth of an idea

What is economics? There are many definitions and many branches of economics but to summarise it in one sentence one can say: 'Economics is the study of the production, consumption and distribution of goods, services and wealth.'

While economics is famous for its complex terminology and hard-to-fathom equations, it is in fact the study of our everyday lives. One of the UK's most famous economists, Alfred Marshall, described it as 'the ordinary business of life'.

The word itself comes from two ancient Greek words: *oikos*, meaning house, and *nomos*, meaning rule or law. Economics can be seen as the study of household management. Of course in today's globalised world it also looks at how these rules work at national and international levels.

A key concept in economics is the scarcity of resources. If land, labour, raw materials, time and brainpower were available without limit, there would be no need for a science of economics. But the fact that all these things – which economists call inputs of production – have a limited supply, means we need a system to decide how to allocate them.

Economics is therefore the science of how those choices are made and the impact they have. Every time someone makes a choice, for instance over whether to spend on a book or a cinema ticket or save the money in the bank, they have to give up the other opportunities. The same applies to a government deciding on a new £10 billion airport or a £10 billion tax cut.

The value of the option that you sacrifice is known as the opportunity cost. Looking at what would be lost by making a choice helps people ensure that it really is the best option and that resources are indeed used most efficiently.

Little and large

One of the first distinctions someone embarking on the study of economics will come across is between micro- and macroeconomics. Like economics itself, these two terms come from Greek: *mikros* means small and *makros* means big. A more modern way of looking at the split is between the 'big picture' of how a national economy works and the 'narrow focus' on how markets made up of many individuals operate.

Microeconomics looks at how individual players in the economy, such as households and firms, interact. It focuses on the impact that their economic choices have on the allocation of scarce resources to meet unlimited demand. These interactions match what one party wants (or 'demands' in economics) and what the other gives in exchange (supply). Each time someone buys a chocolate bar from a newsagent or undertakes the morning paper round, there is an interaction between supply and demand.

The collective weight of all the decisions on demand and supply, use of resources and opportunity costs made by millions of people or firms sets the price for goods, services, assets and labour. Demand and supply therefore form the main principle that underlies all microeconomics.

Macroeconomics, on the other hand, examines the whole economy – the total amount of activity by firms, households and the government. It also looks at how different countries interact with each other through trade and investment. At the heart of macroeconomics is the flow of money around the economy. Households receive wages from firms who receive the money spent by households. Firms and households both pay taxes to the government, which in turn makes social payments to households and pays businesses for goods and services. In an open economy, businesses buy from and sell to firms in other countries.

Added together, these payments make up economic activity, which is often measured as gross domestic product (GDP). Macroeconomists are interested in how fast GDP is growing (growth), how fast prices are rising (inflation), and whether jobs are being created or lost (unemployment).

The challenge governments face is to deliver strong and stable growth, keep inflation under control, ensure the economy creates jobs for its citizens and that households' living standards rise over time. Economists are constantly debating how best to achieve these goals. The main tools are known as fiscal policy,

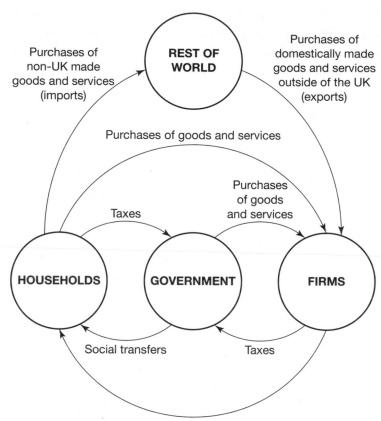

Figure 1.1 How ONS statistics explain the UK economy
Source: Office for National Statistics, UK

which is the role the government can play through taxation and public spending, and monetary policy, where the central bank seeks to control the money supply.

While microeconomics is a fascinating and fast developing branch of economics, this book will focus on macroeconomics as it looks at the issues that readers will come across on the news. Of course macroeconomics uses microeconomics as its foundations, so a basic understanding of the latter is important. By giving a brief history of the key thinkers and doctrines that make up macroeconomics we can see how that building process took place.

A brief history of macroeconomics in 10½ minutes

The man widely known as the father of economics is Adam Smith. Many readers should be well acquainted with him: he has adorned the £20 banknote since 2007. If you have one to hand have a look at his portrait. Once you have got over the fact he was not the finest looking economist, look at the writing underneath: 'The division of labour in pin manufacturing ... the great increase in the quantity of work that results.'

These words are drawn from his major work, *An Inquiry into the Nature and Causes of the Wealth of Nations*, which has provided the foundation for much modern free-market economic thought. He used the example of a pin factory where 10 people all making whole pins might make, say, 10 each a day. By instead getting each worker to do one particular task, such as straightening or cutting the wire, the total number of pins produced will be substantially higher as each one hones their particular skill.

This idea is known as the division of labour and explains why documentary films on economics show workers on a car production line each adding some part to the basic chassis, why busy bankers do not answer the phone themselves but have PAs, and even why we buy pork chops at the shop rather than reliving the BBC sitcom *The Good Life* and rearing our own pigs.

brilliant history

Adam Smith may have been a brilliant economist but he was not the ideal person to know. Stories about his bizarre personal life abound. One says that he became so involved in a discussion with a colleague that he fell into a tanning pit from which he was narrowly rescued. Another has him putting bread and hot water into a teapot and then being shocked at the taste of the 'tea'.

The *Wealth of Nations* is also known for one of the many other ideas that the book generated: the 'invisible hand'. This has become a very handy way to summarise the workings of supply and demand (even though it only appears once in the book). The idea is that everyone in the economy pursuing their own self-interest will eventually produce the most efficient allocation of resources at the right price.

The implication is that leaving the market to itself, rather than any government seeking to control it through rules and regulations, will lead to the best – or optimal as an economist views it – outcome. If one company tries to put up prices without any reason such as higher raw material costs, others will come in at the lower price and take their business until they react. Similarly, if a new need or desire emerges, entrepreneurs will fill the gap.

> markets could regulate themselves and so produce wealth at maximum efficiency

Later free-market economists such as the Austrian Friedrich Hayek were more specific about stating that this 'hands-off' approach in fact works better than any sort of central plan. Perhaps the best anecdotal illustration comes from a question by a Soviet official visiting the UK who asked who was in charge of London's bread supply and was astonished when he was given the answer 'nobody'. This belief that governments should not restrict or interfere in markets because they could regulate themselves and so produce wealth at maximum efficiency forms the basis of the classical theory.

From Marx to Milton via Malthus (and Ricardo)

At one point the intellectual – and sometimes more violent – battle was between classical economists and followers of Karl Marx. The German-born philosopher and economist, who did much of his thinking and writing in London, can be seen as the father of socialism. He argued that capitalism would eventually fail because business owners exploited labour to keep all the surplus value not given to the workers in the form of pay. Such exploitation leads to social unrest and class conflict. To ensure social and economic stability, he suggested, labourers should own and control the means of production. In his view all property is theft (this was the root of the first economics joke I was told. Q: Why don't Marxists drink Earl Grey? A: Because proper tea is theft). At one point half the world's population was governed by nominally Marxist governments. Although the battle between Marxism and capitalism is largely seen as being won by free-market capitalists, his analysis of capitalism's flaws remains relevant and has recently found a new audience.

---

brilliant example

After the global financial crisis hit in 2008, sales of Marx's main oeuvre *Das Kapital* soared as people looked for an alternative to the deregulated free market model that was seen to have failed. In 2011 Terry Eagleton, the British literary theorist, wrote a book called *Why Marx Was Right*. In the book he says that the 'underlying logic' of capitalism remains the same and thus a Marxist critique is still most certainly relevant. In one passage ▶

he writes that to simply accept that 'some people are destitute while others are prosperous is rather like claiming that the world contains both detectives and criminals. So it does, but this obscures the truth that there are detectives because there are criminals'.

Nowadays the main intellectual battle is between monetarists, who are in a way the macroeconomic descendants of the classical school, and Keynesians, who follow ideas originally set out by the British economist John Maynard Keynes. But before we get to that debate it is worth name-checking a couple of other 18th century economists who laid out theorems that are still talked about today.

Robert Malthus, a former priest who became a professor of economics, is known for two things. The first is that he expounded a view that now carries his name: the Malthusian view that the population will outstrip the ability of people to grow enough food to feed the extra mouths. As the food runs short, people will die and the population will fall. While there are always dire warnings about the rise in population, the fact is that the population has jumped from 1 billion in his day to 7 billion now without any sign that food will run out. Advances in technology have ensured that food production has matched the needs of a growing population. But what about the starving millions in Africa, you might ask. A good question, but the sad fact is that there is enough food to feed the world. The problem is with local systems of agriculture and distribution – more of an area for microeconomists.

The second fact for which he is best known is that his population theory led to economics being branded by the writer Thomas Carlyle as the 'dismal science'. But he also left behind other strands of thinking. One element of his gloomy food outlook was an idea now known as the law of diminishing returns. This law states that if you have a fixed productive asset such as land or a factory then each extra worker that is added will increase the amount produced but will eventually decrease the amount each individual worker makes. The point of diminishing returns is reached when individual productivity drops and the cost of producing each extra unit goes up.

Taking a more up-to-date example, a sandwich shop owner can take on another member of staff to help meet extra demand but at some point he will run out of space for workers to make sandwiches without getting in each other's way. The answer is therefore to invest in technology (as with Malthus's food forecasts) or buy the next-door shop.

Malthus also pursued a line of thinking that had a much greater impact than he would have expected. He disagreed with the thinking at the time that demand in the economy created its own supply and that there could never, therefore be an oversupply of products. Malthus disagreed, and said that there could be a glut of goods such as food, and by extension of workers. His solution was to advocate public works and the production and consumption of luxury goods during times of acute depression – an idea that found a new voice a century later.

David Ricardo was a contemporary and friend of Malthus – he helped develop the law of diminishing returns – and was influenced by Adam Smith. Although he made a personal fortune on the financial markets and devoted his early writing to that, like Malthus his writing on macroeconomics was largely based around agriculture. Much of his writing about how income is divided between workers' wages, landlord's rents and owners' profits became an integral part of classical economics. Taking the limited growth potential of any national economy as a given, Ricardo concluded that a particular social class could gain a larger share of the total product only at the expense of another. He also identified how prices over the short term were determined by supply and demand.

The two theories for which he is best remembered are looked at later in this book. He set out the overarching theory of 'comparative advantage' (Chapter 10). This showed why every nation should specialise in the production of those goods it can produce most efficiently and should import everything else from other countries that make them more efficiently. The net result is a growth in world trade and is the underpinning justification for open and free trade. He also stated that extra government spending that is funded by borrowing will not stimulate the economy because consumers and businesses realise they will pay for them in the long run through higher taxes. This theory, known now as Ricardian equivalence, is used to argue against government stimulus measures in times of recession but, as we shall see in Chapter 6, is hotly debated.

The next stop in this line of thinking from Smith to Ricardo should be Milton Friedman, the US classical economist who is best known for developing the quantity theory of money that is the heart of monetarism. But first we need to learn about one of the other giants of modern economics, John Maynard Keynes.

Fight of the century: Keynesians vs Hayek

The debate between classical economists or monetarists and Keynesians will appear frequently during the rest of the book as they are the two main schools of thought. Indeed, one of the oddest features to outsiders about the discipline is that economists at the highest levels of the profession can disagree profoundly. Although economics is a science and uses strict testing processes to prove or disprove theories, no other science can boast Nobel laureates who vigorously disagree with each other! Gunnar Myrdal, a

> monetarists and Keynesians are the two main schools of thought

socialist firebrand, shared the prize in 1974 with Friedrich Hayek. This provoked the joke that economics is the only subject in which two people can share a Nobel prize for saying opposite things. Indeed, Myrdal complained that a prize that could be won by Hayek should be abolished.

---

brilliant example

The power of 20th century economic thinkers such as Keynes and Hayek to exert their influence down the decades can be shown by the popularity of two films made by a TV company called EconStories. The films, *Fight of the Century* and *Fear the Boom and Bust*, have actors playing the two economists debating their arguments in rap verse. Rather than demeaning the debate, the 2010 videos are excellent 10-minute summaries of the debate over the stimulus measures enacted by President Obama a year earlier aimed at averting a Depression. There are probably few other raps that have used the words 'equilibrate', 'regression' and 'self-regulation' in rhymes. Economists interested in demand as a measure of value should note the 6.6 million views they had had by early 2013. A link to the videos can be found at the end of the book.

Since the global financial crisis and recession intensified in 2008 and 2009, this disagreement has been played out at the highest levels over how governments and central banks should respond to the downturn. Keynesians believe that the government can and should play an active role in supporting the economy during a downturn. When businesses and consumers have stopped spending in the face of unemployment and weak demand, they say that the government and central bank should step in to fill the breach. This includes cutting taxes and increasing government spending when the economy becomes stagnant. Equally they advocate raising taxes and slowing spending when the economy becomes overly active, as Malthus indicated 100 years before. The aim in a downturn is to stimulate the economy back towards full employment, known better as stimulus policies. This is also called demand management and – as we shall see – contrasts with supply management favoured by classical economists.

Classical economics rejects the idea that government intervention is beneficial and says that the state should adopt a 'hands off' approach. The argument is that any attempt by the government to push the economy back to full employment will simply reduce the ability of the private sector to sort out the problems and correct the imbalances that led to the crash. The problem with government taking on the job of steering the economy is that it will lead to resources allocated towards political rather than economic goals. Furthermore, classical economists said, the doctrine of Ricardian Equivalence means the stimulus efforts will fail. Instead they propose cutting government spending on goods and services, which will leave room to allow the private sector to expand and create jobs. This has become well known as austerity and by economists as 'expansionary fiscal contraction'.

The events since the crisis began have seen both theories put into action. In the wake of the collapse of Lehman Brothers, in 2009 governments intervened to bail out failing banks, rescue key industries such as the automobile sector in the US, and inject several billions of pounds, euros, dollars and yen. But as the major economies remained stuck in recession or anaemic growth and as the scale of the debts taken on to fund the bailouts became apparent, attention shifted towards more classical attempts to revive the economies. Europe in particular has focused on the need to reduce the government's debts by cutting public spending and raising taxes.

🔍 brilliant explanation

The divergence between these schools of thought comes back to that central idea of supply and demand. Keynes said that firms will not change prices significantly in the short run (due to fixed long-term costs such as wages and supply contracts) so that if consumers and firms cut their spending this would lead to a fall in overall demand in the economy but little fall in prices. Classical economists, however, maintain that the price mechanism, particularly for wages, will be flexible enough to restore the economy to its full employment level.

Show me the money

Keynesian theories dominated economic policy management after the war as politicians believed that they could regulate the speed of growth and counteract recessions by cutting or raising the amount of government spending while the central bank moved interest rates up or down. However, the 'stagflation' experience of the 1970s where growth often fell while inflation rose, making it impossible to pursue the expansionary policies Keynesian would dictate, undermined confidence in the theory.

Milton Friedman, a US economist working at the strongly free-market-oriented University of Chicago, stepped in with a new way of looking at the economy – via the money supply. He revised an earlier theory known as the quantity theory of money that, using excessive simplification, says that the prime cause of a rise in inflation is an increase in the money supply. To control the economy policymakers should therefore target and control the money supply, a policy known as monetarism. This was put into practice by Margaret Thatcher in the UK and by Ronald

> to control the economy policymakers should target and control the money supply

Reagan in the US. Like Keynesianism it ran into its own problems, and today no major central bank directly targets money supply data in setting interest rates.

Another key contribution to the debate came from Robert Lucas, another member of the Chicago school, who developed the idea of 'rational expectations' – the idea that people look ahead and see through the short-term impacts of policy changes to the long-term consequences. For instance, if consumers come to a rational view that ramped up government spending will lead to inflation in the long run, they will alter their behaviour to take account of that. The net effect will be to neutralise the stimulus effect the stimulus measure was meant to have.

↗ brilliant explanation

As well as monetarism, Milton Friedman, who died in 2006 aged 94, contributed one of the most significant economic ideas of the last century – the permanent income hypothesis, which says that households try to smooth out their spending over time based on how much they expect to earn. They will save money when times are good to ensure they have reserves for the lean times. It also means that a temporary jump in income, such as a lottery windfall, will not flow directly into spending. On the other hand, a permanent increase in wealth will have an impact as people can see that raising their lifetime income.

The battles of the last century have become less heated following the collapse of communism in the Soviet Union and the shift towards a market economy in China on the one hand, and concerted efforts by economists to build bridges between Keynesians and monetarists on the other. Chapter 3 looks at the debate more closely but for now it is enough to say that up until the financial crisis at least there was something of a consensus. Monetarists accepted that it was not enough to focus on the money supply and that demand mattered. Similarly Keynesians have acknowledged that the supply side of the economy and the money supply do play a role.

The global financial recession has put economics back in the spotlight and has forced many leading practitioners to look again at the way they view the subject. This will continue to create new theories and new ways of thinking, especially as economists look to other disciplines such as social sciences, business and psychology and even biology to gain a greater understanding of how economies work. In the meantime it is time for us to go back to basics and make our first stop: economic growth.

 brilliant recap

- The global financial crisis has put economics centre stage.

- Economics looks at how scarce resources are allocated amid unlimited demand.

- Microeconomics looks at how individual players in the economy such as households and firms interact.

- This book focuses mainly on macroeconomics which looks at how whole country economies operate.

- The classical school sees economies as self-regulating and believes government intervention can only make things worse.

- Keynesian economists believe that when demand falls and unemployment rises, government intervention is needed to get the economy back to health.

CHAPTER 2

The miracle of growth

'Once one starts to think about [growth], it is hard to think about anything else.'

Robert Lucas, economist, 1995 Nobel laureate

f there is one goal that economists strive to achieve, it is to understand the causes of faster economic growth. Open a newspaper or switch on to a news programme on the television and radio, and the chances are good that there will be a debate over current levels of growth whether in a particular country or for the world as a whole. We continually read or hear numbers such as 0.1% quarter-on-quarter growth, 2.5% growth annualised or 3% annual growth without always knowing exactly what they mean.

But why is growth so important when there are so many other things we could worry about? The simple answer is that citizens of countries that are enjoying economic growth will see increases in their standard of living and thus quality of life. Fast growing countries will see higher levels of national income and more people in work. Policies that permanently increase a country's rate of economic growth are particularly valuable, because the gains get larger and larger over time.

brilliant fact

According to the Institute for Fiscal Studies the benefits of continuous growth over the long term can be truly staggering. If real income - which means taking out the effect of inflation - in the UK grows at 1% a year, it will double in 70 years; if it grows at 3%, it will double in only 24 years.

▶

It is therefore important to understand what drives economic growth in order to make sure that politicians and financial experts in governments and international bodies know what to focus on in order to deliver more of it.

Ingredients of growth

A broad majority of economists agree that economic growth is driven by four primary factors:

- physical capital
- human capital
- natural resources
- improvements in technology (knowledge)

Thinking about those in more detail, physical capital comprises the man-made resources that are needed to produce goods and services. This can include plant and machinery for manufacturers, computer equipment in many offices, the tools needed to operate that equipment and the property needed for factories, offices, schools, hospitals, government and so on. Human capital – or people, in plain English – is an economist's term for the knowledge and skills that workers acquire through education, training and work experience. As with physical capital, human capital raises a country's ability to produce goods and services. Natural resources include energy sources such as coal, oil and gas as well as renewable resources such as trees but also sun, wind and waves.

Perhaps most important is the technological innovation that helps us become efficient at producing goods and services. This includes everything from the provision of clean running water, through to the railways and more recently 4G mobile telecoms capabilities. Other economists have highlighted the importance of strong institutions and the rule of law as an ingredient for growth, pointing to the stark contrast between poverty-stricken North Korea and fast-growing South Korea. However, because different groups benefit from different institutions in different ways, how those institutions develop depends on political rather than economic power. Others have pointed to the different growth rates seen in countries with temperate versus tropical climates.

brilliant example

The US academic economist Robert Gordon often challenges his audiences to take part in a thought experiment. They are given a simple choice. They are allowed to keep 2002 electronic technology, including a Windows 98 laptop accessing Amazon, and can keep running water and indoor toilets; but cannot use anything invented since 2002. The alternative is to have everything invented in the past decade right up to Facebook, Twitter and the iPad, but to give up running water and indoor toilets. This means hauling water into your home and carrying out the waste. Even at 3am on a rainy night, the only toilet option is a muddy walk to the outhouse. Which option would you choose? Gordon says that almost everyone picks the first choice, recognising that just one of the many late 19th century inventions is more important than the portable electronic devices of the past decade on which they have become so dependent.

How fast you've grown!

So having established that economic growth is a vital ingredient to our wellbeing, the next step is to measure it so that we know when the economy is growing. Most people could probably say at any given time whether the economy was growing and at what sort of pace, based on how their income is rising, whether their friends are doing well, whether the value of their home is rising and many other facets of life. This could be seen as akin to putting your finger in the air to gauge the wind direction and speed.

But as *Brilliant Economics* will show, knowing the speed of economic growth is important for a lot of other economic decisions that have to be made. In the meantime it is worth focusing on one measure of economic growth – the gross domestic product or GDP. While it sounds technical it actually means what it says: product because it measures the value of all goods and services produced; domestic because it excludes income from possessions and investments overseas; and gross because it does not distinguish between various uses such as new immediate consumption or replacing worn-out assets. It is therefore the total market value of all final goods and services produced within a country in a given period of time. Not everyone agrees that GDP is a good idea or a good measure. At the end of this chapter we will look at other ways of measuring a country's economy.

> not everyone agrees that GDP is a good idea/good measure

brilliant fact

GDP was created by the US Commerce Department at the height of the Depression in the 1930s and used first as a gauge for production capacity during the Second World War by British economists including John Maynard Keynes. Given the task of determining whether the war was economically viable, they came to the conclusion that war could be good for the economy in that it would have a positive impact on the national growth rate.

When it comes to totting up all the bits in the economy there are, confusingly, three different ways of measuring it – although they should all in theory come to the same figures. One is the output approach that measures what all the different sectors of the economy are producing. This is often used to show how different sectors of the economy are performing. The UK's Office for National Statistics divides the economy into 10 sectors. These sectors (with their 2009 share of the economy in brackets) are: agriculture (0.6%), mining and quarrying (2.4%), construction (6.8%), manufacturing (10.5%), public utilities (1.5%), water supply (1.2%), distribution, hotels and restaurants (14%), transport, storage and communications (10.6%), business services and finance (29.1%), and government and other services (23.3%).

These data confirm the common perception that the UK, like many modern developed countries, is a services-based economy – providing more than three-quarters of output. Those last four sub-sectors amount to 77% of the economy, of which business services and finance, that includes sectors such as banking, insurance and law, is the single largest with almost 30% of the economy. This is three times the size of the manufacturing sector, which has fallen by more than half since 1990 when it made up 22% of economic output.

The income method calculates how much all the various players in the economy have earned. As it suggests, the income approach adds up all income earned by resident individuals or corporations in the production of goods and services. Finally there is the expenditure method, which adds up the money spent by private consumers, consumption by the government, investment, and the difference between what we spend on imported goods and services and what foreigners spend on what we produce. This is the most frequently used and has the advantage of coming with its own easy-to-remember equation:

$$GDP = C + G + I + (X - M)$$

On this basis in the UK in 2011 consumer spending (C) made up around 63% of GDP, government expenditure (G) 23% and investment (I) 15%. As we run a trade deficit the difference between exports (X) and imports (M) took around 1% off growth. The result is a – usually – big number expressed in pounds, euros, dollars or the relevant national currency that represents the size of the economy over a year. In 2011 the UK economy was valued at £1,519,134,000,000 or £1.52 trillion. The pure total indicates which are the biggest economies in the world. By dividing the total GDP by the number of people gives GDP per capita, which is better at showing how rich members of different countries are but also shows how productive different countries are. As Table 2.1 shows, the identities of the biggest economies (most of the rich countries) and the smallest by GDP (Pacific islands) might not come as a surprise; it is noticeable that none of those names appears in the list of countries ranked according to GDP per head. This figure indicates how wealthy each citizen in that country would be if the total wealth were divided up. This can be driven by unusual factors such as huge oil resources (Norway, Qatar) or tiny populations (Luxembourg, Macao).

While the total amount of economic output tells us how large a country's economy is, it does not tell us whether it is growing and, if so, at what rate. In order to know how fast an economy is growing, statisticians take the GDP for one year and compare that with the previous year's output. So if the economic output was $1,000,000,000 one year and $1,003,000,000 the following year then it would have grown by 3%. This is known as 'nominal' GDP, from the Latin word meaning 'number'. The problem is that if prices rise this will look like economic growth even if no extra value has been added to the economy.

Table 2.1 GDP

(a) Total GDP in US dollars (2011)		(b) GDP per capita in US dollars (2011)	
Top five		Top five	
United States	15,094,000	Luxembourg	115,038
China	7,318,499	Norway	98,102
Japan	5,867,154	Qatar	92,501
Germany	3,570,556	Switzerland	80,391
France	2,773,032	Macao SAR, China	65,550
Bottom five		Bottom five	
São Tomé & Principe	248	Sierra Leone	374
Palau	180	Malawi	371
Kiribati	178	Liberia	281
Marshall Islands	174	Burundi	271
Tuvalu	36	Congo, Dem. Rep.	231

Source: Adapted from World Bank, World Economic Indicators Database, 18 September 2012

Imagine a handbag maker produces 5,000 pieces a year. If it sells them at £100 a bag the company will earn £500,000. If it puts its prices up to £110 and manages to sell the same number it will have generated £550,000 even though there has been no increase in economic activity. To counter that, statisticians subtract the rate of inflation from the growth figure to come up with 'real GDP', which is the numbers you read in the newspaper. For example, if nominal GDP growth is 3% but inflation over the year was 1.5% then real GDP growth was 1.5%. Growth is measured officially every quarter so you can see what has changed over the last three months (quarter-on-quarter growth) and how that compares with the same period in the previous year (year-on-year). The United States also uses an annualised growth rate: the value that would be registered were the quarter-on-quarter rate of change to be maintained for a full year. For instance if the quarter-on-quarter growth rate was 0.5% then the annualised rate would be 2.0%. The point is to make sure you understand what the figure is telling you – especially if you want to compare it with other countries.

↗ brilliant explanation

Economists have to cope with an alphabet soup. GDP stands for gross domestic product, which as we have seen represents the total amount of goods and services produced within a country over a year. Gross national product (GNP) includes income from activities owned by citizens of that country in overseas locations. Net national product (NNP) excludes money spent to replace worn-out assets (known as depreciation by economists). Gross national income (GNI) subtracts indirect business taxes. Gross domestic income (GDI) measures total incomes earned by households by summing wages and salaries, rents, profits, interest, and other income.

Different speeds

There is a wide range of rates of economic growth around the world. Countries that have enjoyed a sophisticated economic structure for a long period of time tend to have moderate rates of growth. This includes most of Western Europe, North America and Japan – particularly the G7 group of the world's richest countries (Canada, France, Germany, Italy, Japan, the United Kingdom and United States). These are often known as 'developed' or 'advanced' countries. Countries that have the fastest growth rates tend to be those that have embarked on a major economic change, such as industrialisation or urbanisation. A strong example of that trend is the rapid growth rates seen in Brazil, Russia, China and India, which were given the collective name of BRICs by economists at Goldman Sachs. Since then other groupings have been identified, such as MIST (Malaysia, Indonesia, South Korea and Turkey) and MAVINS (Mexico, Australia, Vietnam, Indonesia, Nigeria and South Africa). These are known as 'middle income' or 'emerging' countries. The idea that countries that start off poor tend to grow more rapidly than countries that start off rich is known as the 'catch-up effect'. Finally there is a group of countries that have very low levels of economic output. These are often called 'developing' economies. As they start to display strong growth – as has happened recently in many sub-Saharan African countries – it must be remembered that these are measured against a low base of economic activity and it may therefore take several years or even decades of strong growth for them to leapfrog into the emerging category. For example, South Korea was one of the poorest countries in the world in the late 1950s. However economic growth of 8% a year between 1962 and 1989 – almost three decades – enabled it to become the 15th richest country now.

> there is a wide range of rates of economic growth around the world

Four times a year the International Monetary Fund, a global organisation, works to improve the economies of its 188 country members, produces estimates of the latest year's growth and forecast for the following few years (we will meet the IMF again in Chapter 8). Table 2.2 gives a snapshot of the IMF's assessment for 2012 and forecasts for 2013. Note the number of minus signs for annual economic growth in 2012 for several European nations and the gap between the average 1.3% growth rate for advanced economies and the 5.3% growth rate for emerging and developing economies.

Table 2.2 IMF World Economic Outlook, October 2012

	Year over year			
			Projections	
	2010	2011	2012	2013
World output	5.1	3.8	3.3	3.6
Advanced economies	3.0	1.6	1.3	1.5
United States	2.4	1.8	2.2	2.1
Euro area	2.0	1.4	-0.4	0.2
Germany	4.0	3.1	0.9	0.9
France	1.7	1.7	0.1	0.4
Italy	1.8	0.4	-2.3	-0.7
Spain	-0.3	0.4	-1.5	-1.3
Japan	4.5	-0.8	2.2	1.2
United Kingdom	1.8	0.8	-0.4	1.1
Canada	3.2	2.4	1.9	2.0
Other advanced economies	5.9	3.2	2.1	3.0
Newly industrialized Asian economies	8.5	4.0	2.1	3.6
Emerging market and developing economies	7.4	6.2	5.3	5.6
Central and eastern Europe	4.6	5.3	2.0	2.6
Commonwealth of Independent States	4.8	4.9	4.0	4.1
Russia	4.3	4.3	3.7	3.8
Excluding Russia	6.0	6.2	4.7	4.8
Developing Asia	9.5	7.8	6.7	7.2
China	10.4	9.2	7.8	8.2
India	10.1	6.8	4.9	6.0
ASEAN-5	7.0	4.5	5.4	5.8
Latin America and the Caribbean	6.2	4.5	3.2	3.9
Brazil	7.5	2.7	1.5	4.0
Mexico	5.6	3.9	3.8	3.5
Middle East and North Africa	5.0	3.3	5.3	3.6
Sub-Saharan Africa	5.3	5.1	5.0	5.7
South Africa	2.9	3.1	2.6	3.0

Source: Adapted from IMF, World Economic Outlook, October 2012, Table 1.1

The table shows clearly how growth rates can vary wildly between countries and over time. While in the table the UK is forecast to shrink by 0.4% in 2012, just five years before, in 2007, it posted growth of 3.0%. Even China saw a slowdown over the same period from 11.9% to 7.8%. While constant and unending strong rates of economic growth would deliver the sorts of expansion highlighted earlier, that pattern

> economies tend to move between boom and bust

seldom happens. This is because economies tend to move between boom and bust, or at least between faster and slower periods of growth. These are known as business cycles.

Circular pattern

Just as the feet of a cyclist go through four phases on each revolution of the pedal, so economists have identified four phases of an economic core business cycle. Starting at the bottom, the first phase is one of expansion. Consumer spending and borrowing rises, output from factories and businesses increases and prices, shares and wages follow suit. But the activity eventually hits a peak, which is the second phase. At this point the economy overheats and, as we shall see in Chapter 7, the authorities will tend to raise interest rates. This higher cost of borrowing will make debts unaffordable and financial markets start to fall. The economy falls into recession, the third phase, which means that business activity, wage growth, house prices and share values all fall. At last the pedal goes past the bottom of its cycle and recovery can begin, so starting the cycle on a new journey.

Developed economies have gone through frequent and sometimes deep business cycles since the early years of the 19th century. However starting in the mid-1990s, many developed economies enjoyed a period of consistently strong growth and low inflation that became known as the Great Moderation.

During that period many economists said that the business cycle might have ended. Robert Lucas, the Nobel laureate economist quoted at the start of this chapter, told the American Economic Association in 2003 that the 'central problem of depression-prevention [has] been solved, for all practical purposes'. During the first decade of this century former British finance minister Gordon Brown frequently claimed that the UK would 'not return to the old boom and bust'.

The period following the financial crisis of 2007/08, where there were sharp falls in growth across the world and downturns in many countries, has become known as the Great Recession. A recession is often defined as two quarters of successive quarter-on-quarter negative growth. In the wake of the global financial crisis the UK had suffered two periods of recession by the end of 2012. However this is nothing compared with Japan, whose economy has moved between contraction and recovery on a regular basis over the past 20 years.

How to grow growth

Given that economic growth is so central to improving people's living standards, achieving faster and more stable growth is one of the highest priorities for governments. There are many elements that can contribute towards growth but a good start is to think about the four engines of growth: physical capital, human capital, natural resources and technological innovation.

A focus on physical capital means ensuring that the basic infrastructure is in good shape, whether that's having enough plant and machinery for businesses to use, high quality public infrastructure such as road and rail transport, or – less visible but equally important – things such as good supply of energy and telecommunications.

The quality of human capital depends on ensuring good quality provision of health and of education and training.

A healthy population will live longer and be able to be active members of the workforce for longer. Overall education is at least as important as investment in physical capital. A well-educated workforce will be able to produce a greater amount of wealth for each hour of work that they do – an idea that economists call productivity. A skilled workforce is essential for taking advantage of new technologies and innovations. In the US figures show that each extra year of schooling raises a person's wage, on average, by about 10%. Thus, one way the government can enhance the standard of living is to provide education and encourage the population to take advantage of it.

This flows into the need to foster technological innovation as higher quality human capital is essential for taking advantage of new technologies and innovations. This is why governments often use tax incentives to encourage firms to invest in research and development (R&D) and to encourage innovation both within businesses and within universities. While natural resources are less important to developed economies than to developing countries, they are still important to an economy. This is highlighted by the discoveries of shale oil made by the United States, which means it will be the world's largest producer by 2017. The importance of technological innovation highlights the need for governments to support innovation.

Because of the ups and downs of the business cycle, economists like to a use a measure of growth that smooths them out. This is known as the trend rate of growth and is roughly the average speed at which an economy has grown over a number of decades. For example, in the UK, the trend rate has tended to be about 2.5%, while US trend growth is considered to be 3% and China is estimated at 7–8%. The gap between the trend and the actual growth is an indication of where in the cycle the economy is. Economists call this the output gap: countries that are growing below potential are likely to have higher unemployment and lower inflation while those growing faster than their historical trend are likely to have the opposite features.

Rethinking growth

While a slight movement in the estimate of GDP growth can move financial markets and dominate news headlines, it is far from a perfect measure of economic activity. The major criticism is that it fails to capture many positive contributions to society and captures some that many people find unwholesome. The manufacture of weapons and of cigarettes is included in GDP through their contribution to manufacturing. The oil and gas sector creates pollution as well as economic output, but while the latter is recorded, the former is not. Because GDP does not include goods and services that consumers do not pay for, it does not count the value of activities that are essential for households such as domestic cooking, babysitting by grandparents and generally serving and helping other members of the household. In 2002 the UK's Office for National Statistics said that if housework were paid, it would be worth £700 billion to the UK economy (more than £900 billion today).

> estimate of GDP growth can move financial markets and dominate news headlines

brilliant quotation

'Our gross national product counts air pollution and cigarette advertising, and ambulances to clear our highways of carnage. Yet it does not allow for the health of our children, the quality of their education, or the joy of their play. It measures everything, in short, except that which makes life worthwhile.'
Robert F. Kennedy, 18 March 1968

But the two key omissions from GDP are any estimate of wellbeing or happiness and any account of the cost to future generations of economic activity today. Even the inventor of the

GDP, Simon Kuznets, who later won the Nobel Prize for his work, was worried from the start that it might lead to a nation's economic activity being mistaken for its citizens' overall wellbeing.

The idea of measuring happiness as well as – or instead of – GDP is gaining in popularity. The concept of Gross National Happiness was adopted by the Kingdom of Bhutan to replace GDP in the 1970s. The New Economics Foundation, a UK think tank, has produced its own national accounts of wellbeing that assess 22 countries using indicators for personal wellbeing, which includes a range of ratings of people's happiness, and social wellbeing to gauge the value that people put on their relationships with others. In an assessment produced in 2009 it found that that the UK ranked 13th for personal wellbeing and 15th for social wellbeing.

In 2008, then-French President Nicholas Sarkozy recruited Nobel prize-winning economists Joseph Stiglitz and Amartya Sen together with French economist Jean-Paul Fitoussi to form a special commission on the measurement of economic performance and social progress. In 2010 the ONS launched a Measuring National Well-being (MNW) programme to provide a fuller understanding of how society is doing than economic measures, such as GDP, can provide. In July 2012 the first experimental results found that almost a quarter (24.1%) of people gave a low rating to their life satisfaction, just under half (49.8%) rated their satisfaction as medium while 26% said their satisfaction was high.

The other failing is that GDP fails to account properly for how activities taking place now affect the possibilities of future generations. Estimates of growth give neither a value to the planet's environment nor a cost to actions that harm it. One possibility is to replace GDP with net national product that takes account of the depreciation of current assets, which would capture the impact of climate change. But for now economic growth is the primary focus for economists and GDP its most popular measure.

---

 brilliant quotation

The importance of tracking GDP was well summarised by Nobel laureate Paul Samuelson and William Nordhaus in the 15th edition of their textbook, *Economics*: 'Much like a satellite in space can survey the weather across an entire continent so can the GDP give an overall picture of the state of the economy. It enables the President, Congress, and the Federal Reserve to judge whether the economy is contracting or expanding, whether the economy needs a boost or should be reined in a bit, and whether a severe recession or inflation threatens. Without measures of economic aggregates like GDP, policymakers would be adrift in a sea of unorganised data. The GDP and related data are like beacons that help policymakers steer the economy toward the key economic objectives.'

---

brilliant recap

- Economic growth is the best way to improve living standards.
- Growth is driven by human activity, physical capital, natural resources and technological improvement.
- The main measure of growth is Gross Domestic Product.
- GDP is calculated by adding up spending by households and governments, investment by companies and any export surplus.
- Countries grow at different speeds depending where they are in their long-term economic development.
- There is pressure to come up with better measures of living standards than GDP.

CHAPTER 3

Business cycles – from boom to bust and back again

'Against a background of mounting uncertainty and instability in the global economy, we set about establishing a new economic framework to secure long-term economic stability and put an end to the damaging cycle of boom and bust.'

Gordon Brown, UK Chancellor of the Exchequer 1997–2007. 18 May 1999

I n the bible, the book of Genesis relates how Joseph inter-
prets the Pharaoh's dream about thin and fatty cows as a
forecast of seven years of boom followed by seven years of
bust ending in widespread famine. This must be one of the first
recorded business cycles but clearly it wasn't the last – as the
events of the first 12 years of this decade have shown otherwise.
It may also be a rare example of an accurate economic forecast.

In a perfect world there would be no business cycles, as they
cause a lot of money to be wasted both on the way up and on
the way down. During a boom people tend to make reckless
decisions such as buying shares or property that turn out to
be overvalued or taking on too much debt in the hope that
continued growth will pay back the loans. During a downturn
people are more likely to lose their jobs or their homes, see their
investments collapse in value and struggle to pay back their
debts. But even more damaging is the uncertainty over how
long it will last, whether it will degenerate into a depression,
how many companies will go bust, how far prices will decline,
and how many men and women will become unemployed.

Phases of the cycle

So how does a business cycle work? A good place to start is
with the humble bicycle. Just as the feet of a cyclist go through
four phases on each revolution of the pedal, so economists have

identified four phases of an economic or business cycle. While there are disagreements about the causes of each phase, there is a broad consensus about that pattern.

Starting at the bottom, the first phase is one of expansion. Consumer spending and borrowing rises, output from factories and businesses increases and prices, shares and wages follow suit. But the activity eventually hits a peak, which is the second phase. At this point the economy overheats as rising interest rates make debt payments unaffordable and financial markets start to fall. The economy falls into recession, the third phase, which means that business activity, wage growth, house prices and share values plummet. At last the pedal goes past the bottom of its cycle and recovery can begin, so starting the cycle on a new journey.

> the long-term trend is for economies to grow even as they go through their cycles

Since the cycle takes place over a period of time, a graph of a business cycle comes out as a long wavy line. Each of the big jumps in the graph represents a boom that sees an acceleration in the creation of both jobs and wealth. Similarly, the downward curves represent the recessions when output falls and jobs are lost. But it is significant that each boom takes the economy to a larger size than the one before. So even though the busts may be painful in the short term the long-term trend is for economies to grow even as they go through their cycles.

Booms tend to last longer than recessions, meaning that each recovery begins on a new high. According to the National Bureau of Economics Research there have been 11 cycles since 1945, with the booms lasting almost five years and the recessions just less than one. This is why the recent global downturn which began in 2007/08 is so significant: many economies such as that of the UK have still not regained the level of economic output seen before the bust.

Developed economies have gone through frequent and sometimes deep business cycles since the early years of the 19th century. However, starting in the mid-1990s many developed economies enjoyed a period of consistently strong growth and low inflation that became known as the Great Moderation. During that period many economists, as well as politicians such as Gordon Brown quoted above, said that the business cycle may have been abolished. Robert Lucas, a Nobel laureate economist, told the American Economic Association in 2003 that the 'central problem of depression-prevention [has] been solved, for all practical purposes'.

This complacent outlook was brought to an abrupt end. In the immediate aftermath of the financial crisis of 2007/08 there were very deep recessions in many countries across the world. This period has become known as the Great Recession; as the downturn was steep, but coordinated action by governments prevented a repeat of the Great Depression of the 1930s.

 **brilliant** explanation

Recession

A recession is often defined as two quarters of successive quarter-on-quarter negative growth or six continuous months of decline. However, in the US phases of recession and recovery are defined by the National Bureau of Economic Research as a 'significant decline in economic activity spread across the economy, lasting more than a few months, normally visible in real GDP, real income, employment, industrial production, and wholesale-retail sales'.

The UK suffered five consecutive quarters of negative growth between April 2008 and June 2009 and then three quarters between September 2011 and June 2012. As a result the size of economy at the end of 2012 was still below where it was in 2008. Japan, which is said to have suffered a lost decade of growth, has recorded 31 negative quarters of growth out of 80 over the two decades to autumn 2012.

Finding the cause

In a perfect economic world the economy would operate at full employment, meaning it is operating at full capacity with output and inflation coasting along at a constant level. While this can happen for short periods, at some point the brakes slam on and growth slows markedly or goes negative. So what causes these business cycles to occur? As is often the case in economics there is no one simple answer, partly because business cycles are not regular predictable patterns but in fact occur irregularly and with varying degrees of severity. Some of the contributing factors to the cause and/or to the depth of the cycle are changes in expectations for the future by consumers and businesses, investment decisions by firms, technological revolutions, outside shocks, credit booms, and trends in human behaviour. Often these factors coincide, which makes it hard to disentangle the exact cause. There have also been a number of economic theories that attempt to set out an overarching theory. Let's look at some of the factors that are seen as triggering the end of a cycle and then at some of those theories.

Hitting the brakes

One cause is the decisions by businesses on what investments to make based on their expectations of future sales and profits. When the economy is strong and companies see the outlook turning more positive they invest more in order to take advantage of an expected increase in income. However, after a while, when it emerges that growth will fail to meet those expectations, firms cut back on investment, which has a knock-on effect on the rest of the economy. As firms produce less, they need fewer workers, so employment falls leading to a drop in spending, thereby creating a vicious circle. This may explain the so-called 'dot.com crash' of 2000 when the emerging internet technologies encouraged a vast amount of investment that in turn led to a surge in share prices and a rise in consumer spending. As investors and businesses realised that they had overestimated future sales and profits, they pulled back, putting the process into reverse.

More recently behavioural economists have used the idea of 'animal spirits' highlighted by Keynes – greed and fear – to explain how people's expectations of the future affect business cycles. If people – whether consumers, investors or policymakers – are very confident and optimistic about the future they are likely to spend and borrow more. This may explain 'gazumping' – the ability of a home seller under English property law to take advantage of last-minute offers during a property boom from buyers

> people's expectations of the future affect business cycles

desperate not to miss out on the next round of price rises, thus helping push prices higher. Similarly, if there is a collective fear that the economy is about to slow, people will cut their spending in anticipation of worse to come, so causing and amplifying a recession. The point is that these decisions are spontaneous, hence the animal nature of the term.

A related cause is the way that companies build up inventories – stocks of goods waiting to be sold. During the upturn in the cycle, firms produce large quantities of goods and take on extra workers to carry out the extra work. Companies build up stocks of goods so that they can ensure they meet the demand. However, at the first sign of a change in the outlook, firms react swiftly by cutting production and instead running down their inventories, either causing or accelerating a wider economic slowdown. Although the level of inventory investment is quite small relative to GDP, economists at the Federal Reserve Bank of Cleveland found that movements were quite large relative to the movements in output.

Booms and busts may also be driven by technological and commercial innovations. These can include new scientific inventions, the development of new products or new ways of performing a task. The first company to successfully exploit that innovation will see a boost to their sales and profits. Other firms will swiftly follow suit and undertake major investment, perhaps tying in with the invest boom already discussed.

However the competition drives prices down – the classic law of supply and demand – and some of the weaker players go bust, causing a negative impact on jobs, incomes and spending. Famous examples of this process include the industrial revolution, the railway boom, the arrival of cheap motorcars, and the invention of electricity for domestic use. More recent candidates include the dot.com crash and the current rapid innovation underway in the smartphone and tablet computer industry.

brilliant example

One of the advocates of innovation theory was Joseph Schumpeter, an Austrian economist who talked about 'innovations in the industrial and commercial organisms'. His thinking led him to come up with the phrase for which he is most famous – creative destruction. As new firms flood the market to take advantage of innovations, those that cannot compete because they are not efficient enough go bust thus clearing out or 'destroying' uncompetitive players.

Another potential cause of business cycles that has received considerable focus is the expansion and contraction of access to credit from commercial banking. When interest rates are low consumers and businesses find it easy to borrow because the banks are willing to lend. They build up large amounts of debt which enables them to fund spending and investment leading to job creation. It also compounds the 'feel-good' atmosphere that encourages further borrowing. Eventually increased demand for loans causes interest rates to rise. This discourages new borrowers while encouraging existing borrowers such as homeowners to pay off their debts to avoid the higher interest payments. If inflation rises too high (as we will see in Chapter 5), borrowing and spending slow down, and as the number of debt defaults rises, banks cut back on lending and may themselves go bust. This contraction hits household income, spending and ultimately the wider economic output.

The final cause of the business cycle is an external shock. This can include a spike in oil prices, outbreak of war or international conflict, bad weather such as hurricanes and earthquakes or stricter environmental and safety regulations. The shock will alter how businesses and consumers behave and this will affect output, consumption, investment and employment and wages. An example of this is the boycott of oil exports by Arab countries in the 1970s that triggered a surge in crude prices and a major recession.

brilliant explanation

The financial crisis of 2007/08 can be explained using a number of factors. In one sense it was a credit cycle that saw millions of people taking advantage of 'easy money' to take on too much debt. The financial innovation that led to the creation of new products such as sub-prime mortgages and structured debt instruments may have been an example of an innovative boom and bust. Animal spirits may have encouraged both homebuyers and financial traders to rush to take advantage of the boom and then spontaneously decide that prices had gone too far. Meanwhile it turned out that many banks had built up large inventories of these complex financial products that they could not sell.

Pedalling a theory

Business cycles are a key part of some of the main economics theories we saw in Chapter 1: how you see the economy operating will lead you to have a view about how you believe the economy can rise and fall. While there is a host of theories with exotic names the divide comes down to whether one looks at the 'demand side' of the economy – the spending by consumers, businesses and governments – or the 'supply side' – changes in prices and wages. One starting point is to go back to classical economic theory which says that buyers and sellers will always find the equilibrium point. Any move away from that full employment point is a temporary aberration that will be corrected through the price mechanism without the need for any intervention from government. Recessions will end once prices and wages adjust to a new equilibrium. Any attempt to intervene with monetary policy or fiscal policy will disrupt that adjustment process.

The main alternative to this was put forward by Keynes and so is known as the Keynesian business cycle. This sees the main cause of recessions or downturns as a fall in overall or 'aggregate' demand in the economy because of a lack of spending by consumers, investment by businesses or the government, or in exports. At the heart of this theory is the idea that the economy will not adjust as smoothly as classical economists believe since workers will not let wages fall in response (known to economies as 'stickiness'). Unlike monetarists, Keynesians believe that the economy will not adjust quickly enough to avoid stagnation (see Chapter 1). Unemployment rises because workers will not accept the pay cuts required to price the jobless back into work. So, to bring the economy back to full employment, Government should intervene with monetary

> Keynesians believe that the economy will not adjust quickly enough to avoid stagnation

policy (cutting interest rates or injecting cash into the system) or fiscal policy (tax cuts and increases in spending) – or both. In extreme circumstances a failure to intervene will see stagnation continue to the point of social unrest. The impulse for this fall in demand primarily comes from a decision by businesses or people to cut investment in line with thinking on animal spirits.

⤳ brilliant explanation

The difference between the two main views of the business cycle comes down to the two different interpretations of where the trigger for the end to an economic cycle comes from. Classical economists see fluctuations caused by outside supply shocks known by the technical term 'exogenous' events. Economists from the Keynesian schools and its later version see the problems as coming from the demand side (as we saw in Chapter 1) of the economy because of internal failures or 'endogenous' causes. In 1994 Ed Balls, currently the Shadow Chancellor but then an adviser to Gordon Brown, famously came up with the concept of the 'post-neoclassical endogenous growth theory' that the then Chancellor used. It prompted Conservative grandee Michael Heseltine to retort: 'It's not Brown's, It's Balls.'

Both classical economic theory and Keynesian theory have come in for criticism because of their inability to explain past downturns: the classical theory does not explain the Great Depression and Keynes's theories did not apply to the 1970s recessions. As the two schools of thought worked out how to adapt their theories, this led to a rash of new theories including new classical, neo-classical, new Keynesianism and neo-Keynesianism. The neo-classicists said that people's behaviour was determined by their rational expectations based on their analysis of the economy. An unexpected shock will force people to react by cutting wages and prices until the economy rebalances. Intervention by the government will have no effect because people will take that into account. For instance, if the government borrows money to pump into the economy, people will know that taxes will have to rise in the long run and so will save rather than spend. Keynesians accepted the rational expectations argument but said that prices and wages did not always react and that intervention will work to bring the economy back to its former level.

The most recent version of the theories based on the supply side of the economy (what firms are producing) rather than the demand side (what consumers are buying) is the 'real business cycle theory' (RBC) that was originally put forward by Finn Kydland and Edward Prescott, who jointly won the Nobel Prize for their work. It says that cycles are not caused by moves in aggregate demand as Keynesians believe, but by the technological shocks discussed earlier. A one-off improvement in productivity due to an innovation such as the invention of the railways or internet communications will lead to a pronounced rise in output, investment, employment and consumer spending. A period when there are no innovations will lead to the reverse process. They found that the pace of technological progress explained three-quarters of US business cycles, with surges in innovation causing expansions and periods of stagnation causing recession.

> cycles are driven by shocks to the demand side of the economy

Despite its name, this does not just refer to technology but to any shocks that alter the productivity of the economy. The initial shock will impact on affected businesses and consumers who will cut back on spending and investment. This then ripples out to the rest of the economy as it impacts on sectors and regions that were not directly affected by the initial shock. This alters how businesses and consumers behave and will affect output, consumption, investment and employment and wages. A pertinent but awful example of that is the tsunami in Japan in 2011 which took an initial toll of human life and buildings but then rippled out to other sectors of the economy that were not immediately affected. The point is that these reactions are rational responses to outside ('exogenous') events.

Since this theory rejects the basic Keynesian idea that cycles are driven by shocks to the demand side of the economy, its advocates have fought back. Larry Summers, an economist who later became US Treasury Secretary, criticised the RBC theory saying there was no evidence of the technological shocks, that it ignores the impact on prices and ignores failures in the exchange mechanism – i.e. the way that firms and workers trade with each other. The argument will run and run.

 **explanation**

Cycle lengths

Just as there are many explanations for the existence of business cycles, so there are a number of categories of cycles that tend to be named after the economist who identified them. Given their different timescales they can often overlap:

Kitchin cycle (3–5 years): a lag in information about demand conditions coming back to firms when they produce too many goods. When the firms see inventories stacking up, they cut back on output until the cycle begins again.

Juglar cycle (7–11 years): driven by flows in investments in fixed capital by companies.

Kuznets swing (15–25 years): coined by the same economist who devised GDP (see **Chapter 2**); these are longer-term cycles on major infrastructure spending on projects such road and railways.

Kondratieff wave (45–60 years): also known as a super-cycle – these periods claim to match long-term economic cycles.

Grand super-cycle (70 years +): these are the longest waves and cycles and are mainly applied to financial markets.

brilliant recap

- Business cycles have been around since biblical times and most people alive now have been through at least one.

- There is no one single cause but candidates include over-investment, building up too many inventories, external shocks and technological innovation.

- The financial crisis beginning in 2007/08 can be explained using most of these theories.

- Economists are broadly split between those who see the main problem as a shortfall of demand and those who believe that the main cause comes from outside shocks.

- This will affect how they believe policymakers should react.

CHAPTER 4

Work and wages

'My unemployed father didn't riot.
He got on his bike and looked for
work, and he kept looking 'til he
found it.'

Norman Tebbit, UK Secretary of
State for Employment, 1981–83

Employment is one of the cornerstones of an economy. The more people are in work, the more money comes back to households in the form of wages and the more cash will circulate through the country's shops, restaurants and entertainment centres. When unemployment rises and people lose their jobs, many families are forced to cut back on their spending and as a result more businesses will cut wages or employees – or even go bust – creating a vicious circle of further job losses, falls in spending and business failure.

This is why many governments set out achieving full employment and stimulating job creation as their top political goals. As a result, figures on unemployment become a bellwether for the success of a country's economic policy for politicians, commentators and the news media. In the early years of the new millennium many economies were heading towards record levels of employment. However in the wake of the 2008/09 global recession and the debt crisis in the eurozone, unemployment rose sharply. In the worst affected countries such as Spain, around one in four people were out of work in 2011 and 2012 while for young people the rate was one in two. In the 2012 US presidential election, the unemployment rate became a core issue at the hustings.

> governments set out achieving full employment and stimulating job creation as their top political goals

Employment and unemployment move roughly in synch with the business cycle that we saw in Chapter 2. It is therefore vulnerable to changes in supply and demand in the private sector, and to rises and falls in tax revenues in the public sector. But clearly the market for jobs cannot be left largely to itself in the way that trade in the market for, say, baked beans is. For the large majority of households in the economy, wages or salaries make up by far their major source of income. This has meant that the course of economic development over the last few centuries has seen tensions played out between the interests of workers, employers and the government.

A working definition

On a basic level, employment is when someone is in work and unemployment is when he or she is out of work. Those are definitions that most people would understand. The problem is there are so many different types of employment and unemployment – and other types of activity in between – that we need to understand.

The best starting point is the total workforce of a country. This includes all people aged 16 or over who are in work (employed) or are actively looking for work (unemployed). The rest of the population is deemed to be not currently active and that includes those in school or college, people carrying out household duties, pensioners, people who cannot work due to a disability and those not looking for work. One way of comparing countries is to look at how many people are in the workforce. This is known as the participation rate and is the ratio of the labour force to the working age population, expressed as a percentage.

Employment can then be broken down: into employees and the self-employed; whether workers are in the public, private or third (charity) sector; whether they are employed on a permanent or temporary basis; according to their gender; and finally by age group. Statisticians also seek to divide employees according to the sectors that they work in. The employment rate – the percentage of the labour force in work – allows changes in the labour market to be interpreted in a wider context by allowing for changes in the population. The headline measure of employment for the UK is the employment rate for those aged 16 to 64.

🔆 brilliant example

In the United States, the federal government classifies all employers according to their primary business activity. The North American Industrial Classification System (NAICS) includes 1,170 industries. For example, code 331513 (Steel Foundries) includes the traditional US job of manufacturing steel castings. Code 711510 is for Independent Artists, Writers, and Performers, which comprises 'independent (i.e. freelance) individuals primarily engaged in performing in artistic productions, in creating artistic and cultural works or productions, or in providing technical expertise necessary for these productions'.

Gizzajob!

The internationally accepted definition of unemployment (from the Organisation for Economic Co-operation and Development) is of someone who does not have a job, has actively looked for work in the previous four weeks, and is currently available for work. The ways of looking at whether someone is actively looking for work and also their 'availability' means there is scope for differences between countries. There are also different ways of doing the measuring. The two main options are carrying out surveys of a representative group of households and counting the number of people claiming jobless benefits. For example, in the UK, the unemployment figure is based on the Labour Force Survey while the claimant count is the number of people claiming unemployment benefits, currently known as Jobseeker's Allowance. Unemployment figures tend to be higher than measures of claimants. This is because the latter excludes many people who want to find a job and have searched for work but do not pass the test for claiming benefit and so are not counted.

Like employment, unemployment can be broken down although here the most used classifications are according to gender, age group and between long-term or short-term unemployment. Another way of looking at this is to identify what is creating unemployment. In any economy people will find themselves out of work for short periods of time perhaps, such as after leaving college or while they are in between jobs. This is known as frictional unemployment. Some industries tend to employ more people, perhaps on a temporary basis at certain times of the year. For instance December will see the shops of London's Oxford Street take on extra workers while the tourist trade in Cornwall will need only a skeleton staff. This is known as seasonal unemployment. People who choose not to be in work make up what is known as voluntary unemployment.

None of these is immediately worrisome as they reflect short-term, largely predictable patterns. However, when people talk about unemployment they tend to think of longer-term more unpredictable worklessness. When an economy slows, businesses will make job cuts to survive, the unemployment rate will rise. As the economy recovers firms will take on more staff and unemployment will fall. This is known as cyclical unemployment. If we remember the idea of trend growth rates from Chapter 2, when the economy is growing below trend, unemployment will rise, and will then fall when the economic growth exceeds the trend rate.

⚹ brilliant explanation

Despite its name, full employment does not mean that every single person is in work. The mainstream economic view is that it means that unemployment is as close to zero as possible, taking into account people who are cyclically unemployed. However, the late Nobel laureate economist James Tobin insisted that full employment meant 0% unemployed.

The most worrying is structural unemployment, which takes place when people find they no longer have the skills that employers want and are unable or unwilling to retrain. This can be driven by shifts in technologies that make certain skills obsolete. In extreme circumstances where a region is dependent on a redundant skill, intergenerational worklessness occurs where no one in the household is in work and younger members have never been in employment. While this involves terrible social costs to those affected, it has costs to the wider economy as well. The loss of skills and rise in unemployment can become a permanent feature of the economy even after the initial causes of it have disappeared. This is known as hysteresis, after the ancient Greek word for 'later'.

⚹ brilliant example

Losing their job is obviously a personal blow to that person, in terms of earnings, prestige and future job employment prospects. But research has shown that there are wider costs to society in the form of higher divorce rates, increased levels of crime and worse health, which all come on top of the costs the state pays in the form of unemployment benefit. One academic study in the US in November 2012 published in a journal called the *Archives of Internal Medicine* found that repeated job losses may be as damaging to the heath of that person's heart as smoking, high blood pressure or diabetes.

The link between unemployment and inflation

Given the negative consequences of unemployment, it is no surprise that politicians will aim for full employment. However, to most economists full employment does not mean getting the jobless rate to 0% although some have seen that as a desirable target. As the previous section shows there will always be some people out of work at some point in time, whether due to the economic cycle, the season of the year, the cycle of people's careers or because of more long-term shocks.

One common definition of full employment is that everyone in the labour force who is willing and able to work has a job other than those in transit from one job to another. Many definitions add in 'at the market rate' on the basis that anyone not willing to work for the rate of pay on offer is voluntarily unemployed. This raises the whole question of the link between unemployment and wages and inflation more generally.

there will always be some people out of work at some point in time

Under the so-called 'classical' view, unemployment is the result of people demanding wages above the level at which supply and demand says they should be set for a particular job. Advocates of this theory believe that any interference in the market for labour, such as a national minimum wage, collective bargaining through a trade union or restrictions on the ability of employers to make workers redundant, simply create higher unemployment by protecting the conditions of those in work.

Keynesian economists disagree, saying that unemployment is due to a deficiency in demand that the government should intervene to rectify. They say that the cuts in wages that classical economists believe should happen would simply sap demand further. Another criticism of the classical school of thought is that it treats workers like a commodity or raw material that can be bought and sold. They point to the fact that the supply of labour cannot be separated from the actual person (as oranges and lemons can be separated from the market stallholder). This implies a direct, personal relationship between the employee and employer. That relationship tends to be long-term and involve ongoing subordination between the two. Unlike most goods and services, individual workers are very different from each other.

Either way, economists agree that there is some long-term link between unemployment and inflation. Initially there was thought to be a trade-off between unemployment and inflation.

A British-based economist from New Zealand, A.W.H. Phillips, said that the greater the fall in unemployment, the greater the rise in wage increases. This was based on an analysis of almost 100 years of UK data up to the 1950s. This implied that there was a 'natural' rate of unemployment that was consistent with a level of inflation. As a result governments felt that if unemployment was too high, they could intervene with measures to stimulate job creation at a cost of higher inflation. Similarly, high inflation could be combated, albeit with measures that led to higher employment. He gave his name to the Phillips curve that shows unemployment falling as inflation rises and vice versa.

> there is some long-term link between unemployment and inflation

However, the experience of the 1970s, which saw both high unemployment and high inflation (which became known as stagflation), undermined people's faith in any trade-off. Instead, attempts to stoke up the economy did achieve short-term falls in unemployment and rises in inflation. But as workers saw the buying power of their wages eaten up by inflation they demanded higher wages, which firms could not meet before laying off staff.

Economists came up with an alternative concept, which was that there was a level of unemployment which could not be further reduced without fuelling rises in inflation. This was called the non-accelerating inflation rate of unemployment or the NAIRU for short. As there was no direct relationship between the two, there was no simple number. In fact the NAIRU can be different for different economies. Modern policymakers have seen the challenge as reducing the NAIRU by making the labour market more efficient and so able to employ more people without causing inflation to accelerate.

A productive workforce

The measure of the efficiency of a country's or company's workforce is known as its productivity. Economists calculate this by dividing the total amount produced by the number of workers or by the number of hours worked. This tells you much about each worker or how much each worker hour produces which makes it easy to compare different industries, companies and economies. Productivity is often called the holy grail of economic prosperity.

Labour productivity has historically been higher in the US than in most European countries. There are many suggested explanations for this but according to economists the measures needed to boost productivity are called supply-side reforms. This is because they aim to improve the way that workers work and to increase their willingness to work – which is how the concept of supply applies to the labour market – rather than boost demand among employers for staff. In economic terms it is about improving the quality of the 'human capital' that we encountered in Chapter 2.

There are many reforms and initiatives that come under this heading and most require some involvement from the workers, employers and the government. Some of the measures have proved controversial. Perhaps the one that excites the least controversy is the need for better training and education of workers.

Research has shown that investment in education and training raises the skills level of workers and makes them more employable and better able to earn higher wages. It leads to greater productivity and improved ability to use existing technology, and contributes to economic growth. In the longer run it will also increase the amount of innovation, which will also boost growth. The government can use tax incentives to encourage workers to retrain to learn more marketable skills. Workers can decide it makes sense for them to invest in education in order to raise their skills which will lead to higher pay in the future. Businesses have also realised that it is in their interest to ensure that their staff attain new skills. There is a growing trend for employers to organise the workplace so that it becomes a learning environment.

Ensuring a more skilled workforce will also help increase the mobility of labour. If workers can move easily to where their skills are in demand then they are more likely to get work. A lack of mobility has the opposite effect as it means workers are unable to move to take a job. This can contribute to structural employment. The government may need to intervene to make it easier for people to move by providing financial and other types of assistance.

Cutting income taxes should in theory encourage people to work more as they will keep a higher proportion of the money they earn. Tax rates in many countries have fallen over the last 30 years. In the UK for example the highest marginal rate of tax was cut from 83% to 60% in 1979 and as of April 2013 will be cut from 50% to 45%. The basic rate of tax has come down more gently from 33% in 1979 to 20% today. Until 2007 there was a 10% tax rate for the lowest earners in the UK, although that was abolished to pay for a cut in the basic rate from 22% to 20%. In 2013 the Coalition Government proposed giving all workers a tax-free allowance until they earned £10,000 a year.

More controversial is the suggestion that governments should reduce benefits payments in order to encourage people to look for work. If social security payments are too high they will erode any incentive for people to look for work, creating what economists call an unemployment trap. However, reducing or stopping payments to people who don't have the skills needed to find work or when there are insufficient jobs on offer can create hardship.

Another controversial reform is to weaken the power of trade unions to call industrial action and impose conditions on employment. This has taken place in the UK over the last 30 years. During that period the number of days lost to industrial action has fallen and the UK is seen as one of the more flexible economies for employment in Europe. Others advocate labour market reforms that would make it easier for mothers, carers and older people to join the workforce by creating a better balance between employment and family care responsibilities.

---

brilliant example

Since the start of the financial crisis in 2007/08 unemployment has risen but not by as much as many economists had feared. Between November 2010 and November 2012 the economy created 600,000 jobs over a period when the economy did not grow. As a result productivity has fallen sharply as a larger number of people are doing the same amount of work. Economists have called this the productivity puzzle. No one has come up with the perfect explanation. Some say that either the employment figures or the growth data must be wrong. Others say that firms have not wanted to make staff redundant because they are worried it will be difficult to recruit people with the same skills when the economy recovers, as happened in the 1990s. Meanwhile workers and trade unions have been prepared to agree to wage freezes or even cuts rather than lose their jobs.

Wages and salaries

The income that workers receive in wages, salaries and bonuses for their work are an essential element in how an economy operates. The cash coming to households helps fund spending on the high street that underpins corporate profits and employment, creating the virtuous circle described earlier. It also generates money for the government in the form of tax. Since the mid-1950s wages have made up between 50% and 60% of annual GDP.

The pace at which wages and salaries rise is an important indicator for the central bank when it sets interest rates, as higher wages can encourage higher levels of spending that may push up prices. In the UK statisticians publish an average earnings index along with the monthly employment and unemployment figures that shows how fast workers' earnings have risen over the last year.

But how are wages and salaries set? Why do doctors and lawyers earn much higher salaries than teachers and police officers, who in turn earn more than shop staff and dinner ladies? These are tricky questions and many of the great names from Chapter 1 including Marx, Smith and Ricardo have all helped develop various theories. Despite their different roles their wage – which we will use to cover wages and salaries – is the price of their input. That price is set in the labour market by the forces of supply and demand, which set relative wage rates for different jobs and raise wages in line with increases in productivity and national output.

According to early classical theory, supply and demand would settle the wage for a job at the lowest level needed to raise another worker, or a basic subsistence level. The theory, known as the iron law of wages, was based on the idea that any increase in the wage rate above the subsistence level would induce an increase in the birth rate and therefore in the supply of labour. The expanded labour supply would force the wage rate back to the subsistence level. Any decrease in the wage rate below the subsistence level would result in starvation and a reduction in the labour supply.

Fortunately this law no longer applies in developed economies. One of the reasons is that governments increasingly intervene to ensure that wages do not fall to a subsistence level by imposing a minimum wage. The rise of trade unions has arguably raised wage levels.

Supply is determined by many of the factors already mentioned including the participation rate, the number of hours people are prepared to work, the effort they put in – their productivity – and the amount of training they have done and skills they have acquired. Demand will vary according to the type of job, the size of the company or sector and the level of skill required. This is constantly changing, as shown by the shift from mass-employment in manufacturing to a services-based economy built on many different sectors. Each of the occupational categories – unskilled, semiskilled, skilled, clerical, technical, professional, managerial – imply different levels or skills, each containing a wide range of jobs in terms of the skill and training required. This leads to what economists call wage differentials.

---

brilliant example

Income inequalities have risen in recent decades and many critics point to the example of the earnings of a professional footballer and a nurse. While the footballer spends a few hours a year on the pitch, the nurse will work for many hours doing a job most people believe is socially useful. Despite the moral argument, the economics is clear, albeit dismal. The footballer is compensated for committing to a 24/7 regime of training while the nurse's obligations are limited to the working week. More significantly, the footballer creates more revenue for the employer through merchandising, TV rights and ticket sales, which are not options for the nurse. A top-flight footballer is one of a team of 11 and he will have a high level of skill and talent that may be unique.

One of the main reasons why wage rates vary so much is that employers have to take into account a whole range of costs on top of an hourly or annual wage. There are costs involved in hiring and firing someone, including recruitment, training costs for the new recruit, and sometimes severance pay for the departing employee. This creates an incentive for employers to hold onto certain staff. Many turnover costs are related to employee skill level, and employers are more reluctant to lose skilled employees.

> employers are more reluctant to lose skilled employees

Future challenges

The world of work is constantly changing. Jobs that were commonplace half a century ago in Britain and other western economies such as shipbuilding, iron and steel production and the manufacture of shoes have all but disappeared. Sectors that employ large numbers of people, such as IT services, financial derivatives traders and public relations officers, either did not exist or were much smaller. It is certain therefore that the next five decades will see similarly dramatic changes. Most will be impossible to predict but some long-term trends are already clearly visible.

Technology

Innovation in computer technology is constantly changing the way that jobs are carried out. On the one hand computerisation can reduce the need for workers as it enables factories such as car assembly plants to produce the same number of cars with far fewer people even though the staff who do work there are more highly skilled. On the other hand it creates a large number of jobs in new industries such as web development, software design and the design of popular items such as smartphones and tablet computers.

brilliant fact

Mechanisation and automation has resulted in a hollowing out of the labour market in the West. Semi-skilled routine manufacturing and service occupations (such as assembly line workers and bookkeeping clerks) have been outsourced or disappeared from the labour force. Growth in employment of skilled professionals such as financiers and doctors at the top of the income scale and demand for labour in routine low-skilled occupations that computers and machines cannot replace, such as cooking and bus driving, has increased. This has led to an 'hourglass' shaped labour market. In the 13 years to 2006, the number of hours worked in middle-income jobs in the EU fell around 8% but rose by 6% and 2% for low- and high-income jobs respectively.

Ways of working

The era of the job-for-life has ended. Workers coming into the labour market can expect to work for several employers over their career. The nature of work has also changed, from being dominated by jobs dependent on their locations such as factory work, shopkeeping and mining, to jobs that can be done in various locations. The advent of mobile technology and cloud computing means that many jobs can be done in remote locations. It also enables employees to work more from home and for people to set up their own businesses in areas where it is not necessary to have an office. In the wake of the financial crisis there was a rise in the number of people taking part-time jobs or becoming self-employed, although it is not clear whether that was through choice or necessity.

Demographic change

People are on average living longer thanks to healthier lifestyles and breakthroughs in medical technologies. This will put pressure on pensions and healthcare systems as pensioners live for many more years after quitting work than they did in the past. This has led to an increase in the number of people working past the traditional retirement age and that trend is likely to increase. In the 20 years to 2012 the proportion of those aged over 64 in the working population rose from 5.5% to 9%. However it also poses a challenge as it raises what is called the 'dependency ratio'. This is the percentage of dependent people (pensioners and children under 16) as a share of the number of working people. Unless there is a massive increase in the number working past retirement age this will put pressure on the rest of society. Spending on healthcare will rise while tax revenues will be unlikely to grow as fast. As a result working-age people may well have to face higher taxes to make up the shortfall. According to the UK's Office for National Statistics the ratio of the number of pensioners to the working-age population has been constant at around 30% over the last few decades. But it forecasts that it will hit 50% by 2050 unless the pension age is lifted.

Migration

People have always moved to find work in times of adversity. The emigration of almost a million Irish people to the United States to escape the starvation caused by the potato famine is a good example. But three recent events heralded the onset of a global labour market. The fall of the Berlin Wall in 1989 and the accession of China to the World Trade Organisation system in 2001 opened up large parts of the world that previously had been shut out of the global market economy while the global telecommunications revolution brought people closer together (albeit virtually). According to the 2011 Census the number of foreign-born residents in England and Wales has risen by nearly 3 million since 2001 to 7.5 million people.

While this has enabled workers to move for work more easily, especially for new member states of the European Union, the more important phenomenon has been what is known as 'outsourcing'. Companies realised that they could take advantage of cheaper labour in other countries. They could move production facilities overseas while new technology meant that back office functions such as call centres and document processing as well as 'mobile' skills such as web design could be carried out abroad. However this has led to protests among workers in western countries angry at seeing their jobs 'exported' to countries such as China. Recently there has been a trend for companies, particularly in the US, to bring production back home in a trend with the equally ugly name of 'reshoring'.

Summary

All these trends will mean that the nature of work will continue to change, which in turn will have an impact on the make-up of a country's workforce and the rewards that its members will gain from employment. There are also bound to be some other structural changes to the labour market that one cannot yet predict.

brilliant recap

- People are either employed, unemployed, inactive, in education or retired.

- There are different types of unemployment: structural, cyclical, frictional and seasonal.

- Employment can affect inflation through changes in wages but economists disagree about how that relationship works.

- Ageing populations, immigration, technology and ways of working will change what jobs people do.

CHAPTER 5

The pain of inflation

'Inflation is as violent as a mugger, as frightening as an armed robber and as deadly as a hitman.'

Ronald Reagan, US President, 1980–88

No one likes it when prices go up. Having to get more money out of your purse or wallet to pay for the same amount of goods in a shop irritates most people. This is what most of us understand by inflation. But it goes wider than just shop prices and can be applied to many items other than consumer goods – wholesale goods, assets such as houses and even wages.

For an economist, inflation is a persistent rise in the general level of prices. A one-off spike in the price of bread is bad news for families but will not qualify as inflation unless it keeps rising and leads to a wider increase in prices. The prices of different goods and services will rise and fall – although mainly rise – at any point in time. Inflation is therefore best understood as an average rise in all prices in an economy over a particular period of time.

> inflation is a persistent rise in the general level of prices

The inflation figure is very important in economics. It gives a signal of how the economy is performing. If inflation is too high it may indicate that the economy is overheating and if it is very low and has even turned negative – so that prices are falling – that may indicate the economy is heading into a recession or even a depression. The best outcome is that inflation is neither too hot, nor too cold but just right – which is why many people talk of a 'Goldilocks economy' after the well-known fairy tale. This is why governments and central banks continually monitor inflation to see where it might be heading.

What is inflation?

A bit like art, most people can recognise inflation when they see it. It is when prices are going up. Prices can go up and down all the time such as when shops put on special offers or when a sudden heavy shower sees the price of umbrellas in tourist traps go up equally quickly. But to an economist it is a bit more specific. Inflation is a sustained increase in the average level of prices across the whole economy that leads to a decline in the purchasing power of the money in people's pockets. For example, the price of bread could double but if prices overall across the economy do not rise in sympathy then an economist will not 'see' any inflation. As with GDP growth it is most commonly talked about as an annual increase.

History of inflation

In 1913 on the eve of the First World War prices in the UK, overall, were almost exactly the same as they had been at the time of the great fire of London in 1666. According to a website that tracks inflation in the UK since the 13th century (www.measuringworth.com) prices rose by 0.2% a year. In contrast, since 1945 they have risen almost 6% a year. That is not to say there had been no inflation or deflation or inflation over the intervening 250 years. Quite the opposite: a chart of inflation over that period would show a series of sharp spikes in either direction as short periods of inflation are followed by equally brief periods of deflation. Sustained price increases were not prevalent until the 1900s and since the Second World War there has only been one year (2009) when prices fell.

The post-war period saw an era of relatively high and sustained inflation in the West. In the 1970s inflation rose sharply when the Arab boycott of oil exports caused oil prices to spike, which led to a general rise in prices and wages. Inflation also reared its head in the 1980s in the UK as the country saw a major property boom. However, since 1992 inflation has fallen steadily from over 20% to around 2%. This process, which is a good example of disinflation, was the result of a decision by many governments to target inflation (rather than the money supply or exchange rate).

Measuring inflation

In order to track inflation, we first have to measure it. As we saw with growth there is more than one measure. The most commonly used measures are those that track the goods and services that households buy in shops or online. In the UK there are two measures: the retail price index (RPI) and the consumer price index (CPI). For many years the traditional measure was the retail price index. This is still used by the UK government to raise the basic state pension each year. Since 2003 the official measure monitored by the Bank of England has been the consumer price index, which is also used by the rest of the European Union. This is used to increase state benefits, tax credits and public service pensions in line with the cost of living. RPI tends to run faster than CPI as it includes housing costs and because of technical differences between the two.

⟋ brilliant explanation

The basic approach to the measurement of inflation adopted by both the CPI and RPI is the same, but they differ in two key ways. The one clear difference between the two is that RPI includes the costs of housing (mortgage interest costs and council tax) while CPI does not. The ▶

complicated bit is that they use different maths. RPI uses the arithmetic mean familiar to anyone from school: add up all the price rises and divide by the number of units. CPI uses the geometric mean which multiplies the prices of all the items together and then takes the nth root of them, where 'n' is the number of items involved. The Office for National Statistics (ONS) says this better reflects changes in consumer spending patterns relative to changes in the price of goods and services.

Every month government statisticians go around the country 'collecting the prices' of a basket of goods and services that are seen to represent how a typical household spends its money. In the UK price collectors record about 120,000 prices for more than 650 goods and services. These prices are 'weighted' to ensure they reflect the relative importance of the items in the average shopping basket.

brilliant example

The Office for National Statistics revises the contents of its inflation basket every year. In 2012 it removed items such as casserole dishes, stepladders and charges for developing camera film. In their place items were added including tablet computers (such as the iPad) and teenage fiction books (including the *Twilight* series). Looking back, 2003 was the last year when inflation measures included prices of local newspapers and toasters. The first basket in 1947 included wild rabbit and household mangles for drying clothes. However, original items still in the basket include eggs, tea, bread, cigarettes and milk.

This is all boiled down to produce an estimate for how much prices have risen over the last year, whether measured by the RPI or the CPI. In the UK the CPI figure is the one that tends to crop up most often on the news as the government has set a target for inflation of 2%. When inflation is higher than that it may indicate that the economy is running too fast. Equally a figure way below inflation is a signal that the economy is growing more slowly than its potential.

But different people will be interested in different measures of inflation. The main figure, often called the headline index, can be broken down to show how fast the prices of goods or services are rising. Motorists can see how fast petrol and car repair prices are rising, for instance. The ONS also produces indices that take out the impact of tax on inflation.

Because an inflation figure is simply a measure of how prices are now compared with a year ago, they can be applied to many other parts of the economy. Producer price inflation measures the prices of raw materials that factories use, such as the oil and other fuels and various industrial metals. It also measures the cost of goods leaving the factory gate and going on to other manufacturers. There are also a large number of measures of house price inflation. This is the one form of inflation that is more popular as it shows how much the value of private homeowners' properties are rising. However, for people who are trying to get on the housing ladder it is just as pernicious as rising costs in the local shop.

What causes it?

Inflation happens when businesses raise their prices. But what causes them to do that? It is important to remember that prices are set by the level of demand in the economy – how much people want to buy something – and the quantity of supply or how much can be produced. Strong demand will push prices up unless new supplies come on tap to meet that demand. Similarly a sudden drop in the supply will also push prices up as people will have to fight over the smaller amount of goods on the market. Put into reverse and those trends will push prices down.

There are a number of reasons that have technical names but all boil down to how people react to wider changes in the economy. The idea that inflation occurs when demand rises faster than supply can keep up with is known as 'demand-pull' inflation. This begs the question as to why demand rises. Here again there are likely to be a number of reasons but a lot of them come down to the old saying about 'too much money chasing too few goods':

> inflation occurs when demand rises faster than supply can keep up with

- **The economy grows faster**. A period of increased economic activity will see more jobs created, putting more money into people's pockets for them to spend. This feeling of extra wealth will also fuel a rise in optimism for the future that will make people more confident about spending.

- **Government spending spree**. As we saw in Chapter 2, governments are a major contributor to economic growth. When politicians decide to spend more on providing schools, hospitals or better quality roads, for example, this will increase the demand for goods and services as well as putting more people into work.

- **Inflation expectations**. Where consumers believe that, for whatever reason, inflation is likely to continue rising, this will encourage them to spend more money now to avoid having to spend more money buying the same goods in the future. This leads to an increase in demand.

- **Technological innovation**. Occasionally a product comes onto the market that swiftly becomes a must-have item. A recent example is the tablet computer, and particularly the iPad device, while another is the iPhone and other smartphones. In some cases the power of the brand also helps support demand and allows the manufacturers to keep prices high and rising. Going back over time, radios, televisions, cars and dishwashers have all had an impact.

However, the latter examples show that the impact on inflation can be short-lived: once the items become standard, prices are likely to stop contributing to inflation.

brilliant example

Prices of items can fall without causing any wider economic upset. A good example is technology goods where not only do prices fall but more recent versions can do even more than older models. A survey of prices in the United States at the end of the first term of President Barack Obama showed that while over four years prices of shop-bought food had risen 6%, prices of televisions had fallen by 57%.

When a shortage of supply is the main contributor to inflation, this is known as 'cost-push' inflation. Assuming that the demand stays the same, this shortage of supply will mean that prices will rise as the same number of people will be chasing a smaller amount of goods. Cost-pull inflation only happens when people cannot cut back on their use or find alternatives. When people carry on buying goods even when the prices rises, this is said to show inelastic demand. Examples include:

- **Raw materials**. Problems with supplying the materials that are needed to make other goods will push up the price. Natural disasters such as droughts can destroy harvests, driving up food prices. Events such as hurricanes can destroy or damage plants producing important inputs such as steel. Perhaps the most famous example is the boycott on oil exports in the 1970s by a number of Arab countries organised in protest at the West's support for Israel. This restriction of oil supply caused the price to rise sharply, and pushed up inflation steeply in countries such as the UK that were dependent on oil imports.

- **Wages**. If workers are able to demand increases in pay that outstrip the increase in what they produce, then the rise in the wage bill will probably be passed on in the form of higher prices.

- **Government intervention**. Politicians often impose taxes or regulations on activities they believe are harmful. By putting taxes on goods such as alcohol and cigarettes they can raise prices.

- **Exchange rate devaluation**. If the value of your currency falls against those of other countries then companies here will need to use more of their pounds to buy the same goods abroad. If they can they will pass this on in the form of higher prices.

Another explanation is that the supply of money has increased too fast. This could happen because the government has decided to print more money, a policy widely known as quantitative easing, perhaps to combat fears of a depression, as happened after the 2008/09 financial crisis, or to try to create a stimulus to the economy to hold onto power. It could also happen because the strength of demand in the economy is encouraging consumers to borrow more money while banks are happy to lend to them in the expectation that the economy will continue to expand.

Why we need inflation

But if inflation is indeed such a bugbear, would it not be better to get rid of it altogether and aim to keep prices fixed? Economies can function fine without rising prices. This might seem like a good idea and – as is often the case – it takes the logic of economics to show why it is not. As the Bank of England says in its educational materials: 'We prefer to have a moderate amount of inflation rather than zero inflation.'

One reason is that if inflation did go to zero then there would not be much reason for people to rush to spend their money as it would still be worth the same in a year's time. Indeed, at times when prices were falling people would probably hoard their money and wait for prices to fall further. Savers would also have to get used to earning no money on their investments.

Having zero inflation and interest rates would remove a major tool in the Bank of England's armoury in times of a downturn – cutting interest rates. Interest rates can't fall below zero as that would mean lenders paying people to borrow money! One of the weapons that central banks have in times of recession is to set negative interest rates *in real terms*. If inflation is 10% but interest rates are 5% then depositing £100 in a savings account will leave the saver with £105 after a year. However, inflation means that the £105 will be worth less than £100 was a year ago. This encourages people to spend and pull the economy out of a downturn. If inflation is at zero then it is not possible to have negative real interest rates as the lowest rates can go is zero.

> 'we prefer to have a moderate amount of inflation rather than zero inflation'

Similarly, workers would have to get used to their pay never going up. While this would be fine on one level as their wages would buy the same as they did a year ago if inflation is zero, it would be a big culture shock after being used to seeing their wages rise over time. For employers zero wage inflation would remove the option to impose a pay freeze in a downturn, something employers often do to reduce costs until the economy recovers. Instead employers would have to cut wages, which would have a demoralising effect on current employees and make it harder to find new recruits.

Winners and losers

While no one likes to pay more for their shopping, a rise in inflation actually affects some people more than others. This is because of the powerful impact that inflation has on the value of investments, debts and payments. So even assuming we have low and stable inflation, there will be winners and losers.

Winners

The big winners are **borrowers** as their debt is a fixed number of pounds. As inflation leads to a rise in their salary, each year they can pay off part of their debt with money that is worth less than it was a year ago. When inflation rises high enough to be running faster than the interest rate that the borrower must pay, economists call this effect a negative interest rate and it means that borrowers are effectively being paid to borrow money.

Mortgagees with a fixed-rate loan get a further payoff as the interest payments on their home loan will not rise even as inflation rises all around them. Indeed, anyone with a loan with a fixed rate, whether for a business or to buy a car or holiday, will find it easier to pay the interest – and the debt at the end of the loan period.

Sticking with property, **homeowners** tend to feel like winners as property prices often rise during periods of inflation. During the property booms of the late 1980s and in the decade preceding the 2007 crash, there was a popular urban legend of guests at dinner parties regaling each other with stories about how their house had 'made' more money than they had at work.

Savers with inflation-linked savings will be protected from inflation as their interest payments will match the rise in prices.

Investors in commodities are unlikely to lose as the prices of these raw materials tend to track inflation. Indeed, gold is seen by many as a way to 'hedge' against the impact of inflation.

Losers

The immediate losers when there is high inflation are **consumers** as they have to pay more for their weekly shop and on vital services such as electricity, water and gas well before they are likely to see any increase in their salary to match.

The big losers are general **savers**. A lump sum squirrelled away as a nest egg will lose its worth over time as money loses its buying power unless you have the index-linked safety net described above. Savers with a fixed interest rate – which would seem sensible in times of low inflation – will lose as their monthly or yearly payments buy less than they did a year ago.

People on fixed incomes, especially **pensioners**, will also lose out. For people whose sole or main source of income is a fixed payment such as a pension or benefit, the value of their payments will decline in times of

> most people can cope with some inflation especially if they can see it coming

inflation. As we saw earlier, benefits are raised in line with inflation but only once a year and will depend on the snapshot of inflation at that time.

Although **businesses** can put up their prices they are also affected by inflation. As prices rise people will cut back on their spending, and especially for luxury items (known as 'elastic' goods). Rising prices also adds costs to businesses, as they have to spend money on changing their price labels more often.

Variable-rate mortgages holders will see their payments rise in line with inflation.

Inflation extremes

Ultimately most people can cope with some inflation especially if they can see it coming through the pipeline. Households can use simple financial products to hedge against inflation. Savings accounts with variable interest rates will mean that the payments rise as inflation does (even if the real value of the capital does not). More adventurous investors can decide to buy shares in commodity companies. Even braver – and probably wealthier – people can decide to buy esoteric investments such as art, gold or property that many experts believe will leave them better off than leaving the money in their bank account.

brilliant example

One calculation often used by gold bugs – the colloquial name for enthusiastic investors in the yellow metal – shows that in Roman times you could buy a high-class outfit for one ounce of gold, which is worth about £1,000. If you go to a quality tailor today looking for an executive uniform – business suit, shoes, tie and so on – it is likely to cost you £1,000. They say this shows gold can hold its value even over 2,000 years.

Similarly, if deflation and falling prices are on the horizon then a fixed rate savings account will protect interest payments. Bonds – IOUs given by governments and companies – can protect investors as they come with a fixed interest payment.

But the reason people and governments worry about inflation and deflation is that when the economy suffers an extreme version of either it usually leads to a very miserable outcome. When prices rise incredibly fast this is known as hyperinflation and is probably the more famous of the two. But deflation too can be a major worry.

Hyperinflation

In 1919 the price of a loaf of bread in post-First World War Germany was 50 pfennigs or half a Reichsbank mark (RM). A year later it had soared to RM1.20, and the following year hit

RM4. By the middle of 1922 it was RM163 and at the start of the following year it had surged to RM250 a loaf. By September 1923 it was RM1.5 million, rising to RM1.7 billion in October before increasing astronomically to more than RM200 billion in November. German people would go shopping with laundry baskets and wheelbarrows full of increasingly worthless notes and often discover they could only buy half of what they had done the previous day. In the end people resorted to bartering, such as paying for a haircut with eggs.

This is one of the most famous examples of hyperinflation, although there is surprisingly no precise official definition. One economist suggested that it happened when the monthly inflation rate exceeded 50%, and ended when the monthly inflation rate dropped below 50% and stayed that way for at least a year.

In Weimar Germany inflation hit 21% – a day! The immediate cause was the decision of the government to print money faster than the economy was growing – the typical cause of hyperinflation. It should also be remembered that the government did this to meet the huge burden of financial reparations that the Allies had demanded at the Treaty of Versailles. In 1919, when he was just 36, John Maynard Keynes published a book prophetically warning that the treaty would lead to the financial collapse of Germany, which in turn would have serious economic and political repercussions on Europe and the world.

The global accountancy standards body, the IASB, says that hyperinflation happens when the cumulative inflation rate over three years approaches, or exceeds, 100%. Other signs of hyperinflation include people storing wealth in foreign currencies and businesses pencilling in likely price increases into their contracts as well as a trend of people generally using a foreign currency to settle prices.

While Germany may be the most famous example, scholars have tracked many examples of hyperinflation since the Second

World War. The most recent example was in Zimbabwe, where inflation hit a peak of 98% a day – meaning that prices were doubling between dawn and dusk. But the worst outbreak was in Hungary just after the war when the pengo's daily inflation rate hit 207%. This meant that prices rose more than three-fold every day – equivalent to 15% an hour. The monthly infla-tion rate was so high it required advanced mathematics even to express it. The rate of **4.19 × 1016%** means prices were rising by 41,900,000,000,000,000% a month.

Deflation

Compared with those experiences, deflation sounds less perni-cious. Deflation is the mirror opposite of inflation. It is a per-sistent fall in the general level of prices. Of course falling prices sounds like a great idea – remember the example of computers getting cheaper and better at the same time, or the sharp fall in international phone costs thanks to millions of kilometres of telecommunications cables that were laid at the turn of the last century. And if prices were to fall while real income continued to rise then everyone would feel a lot better off. In fact during the industrial revolution in the US in the final decades of the 19th century, advances in industrial technology and the expan-sion of the railways enabled prices to fall even as growth surged. Prices fell because the supply of money did not expand suffi-ciently to meet the higher demand.

⤢ brilliant explanation

It is important not to confuse deflation, which is a persistent fall in the general level of prices, with disinflation, which is a decline in the rate of inflation.

However, most examples of deflation are accompanied by falls in output and employment. For instance, during the Great Depression of the 1920s and 1930s there was a total decline in prices of 26.7% spread over seven years while economic output contracted by 22.5% over five years. The most notable case is that of Japan, which has had bouts of falling prices since the mid-1990s.

Once deflation gets hold of an economy, it can be hard to break free. Once consumers see that prices are falling, they are more likely to delay their spending in the expectation of getting a better bargain in a few months' time. As spending falls, so businesses that make, provide and sell the goods and services contract, see profits fall and cut staff and wages to deal with the falling revenues. As prices continue to fall this becomes a vicious spiral.

It also increases the burden of debt. While the sum of the debt is fixed, as other prices fall it becomes higher in value in real terms. If the interest payments are at a fixed rate then they will be harder to pay as incomes fall. This can lead to debtors defaulting on what they owe which then threatens to bankrupt the lenders. If people with debts such as homeowners decide to sell their property to pay off the debt this can fuel a fall in prices, especially if large numbers of sellers come onto the market at the same time. This too can cause a spiral as other people rush to sell before prices fall. Another reason why deflation is bad news is that it is hard for governments to stem it. Central banks can only reduce interest rates to 0% and if consumers will not borrow at that point, the policymakers have lost the use of one of their main weapons against high inflation.

Both benign and malign deflations are caused by the same situation: the supply side of the economy – its ability to produce goods – grows faster than demand. If this gap is created by an increase in supply, such as during the US industrial revolution, then that is more likely to lead to the benign version. But if it is driven by a fall in demand, caused perhaps by a banking crisis in Japan or by the economic shock from the Great Depression, that is more likely to be the unpleasant type. The government can cause inflation either by reducing expenditure, which takes demand out of the economy, or by raising interest rates, which makes money more expensive and so discourages people from spending.

 brilliant recap

- Inflation is a sustained rise in the general level of prices over time.

- It effectively erodes the buying power of the money in your wallet or purse.

- Its root cause is too much money chasing too few goods.

- When inflation gets out of control (hyperinflation) it can be hard to regain control.

- Deflation, which is the opposite of hyperinflation, can also be hard to reverse.

- Since the early 1990s many economies have enjoyed low and stable inflation rates on average.

CHAPTER 6

The role of government

'Taxes are what we pay for a civilized society.'

Oliver Wendell Holmes, US Supreme Court Justice, 1904

The financial crisis that began in 2008 has put the role of central government back at the centre of economic policy – and into the heart of the debate over how to run an economy. Before the global recession there had been a growing consensus among politicians on both sides of the political divide that the government should not interfere in the running of the economy. Many policymakers have argued that governments only distort the smooth operating of the economic system. Before considering the arguments for and against the greater role of government, it is worth thinking about what it does.

Just another economic actor – but a big one

The government is a major player in the economy of a country. Whether seen as central, regional or local government, the public sector makes up a large share of economic activity. In the UK it has tended to hover around 40% in recent decades. It is much less in the United States, slightly more in Western European countries such as France and Germany (where it has been 40–50% in normal times) and noticeably more in some Scandinavian nations.

Government has a role in the economy in two different ways; through the tax it levies on its citizens and corporations; and the goods and services it buys and people it employs as part of its spending programmes. As will become important later in this chapter, it is important to understand that both these activities change the way the economy operates.

By raising taxes, governments take money from consumers and businesses that they might have saved or used in a different way. By raising or lowering tax rates, governments can influence how people and companies behave. One of the most obvious examples is the duty on cigarettes which makes a packet of 20 much more expensive and has been credited with helping cut smoking deaths in the UK.

Taxman: 'there's one for you, 19 for me'

Paying tax has never been popular, as the lyrics to The Beatles' hit some half a century ago show. Tax has been a long-standing theme in history. Jesus urged his followers to 'render unto Caesar what is Caesar's', while as the American statesman Benjamin Franklin noted 200 years ago, the only things certain in life are death and taxes. Excessive taxation has often been identified as a cause for major public protests in Britain, including the noblemen's rebellion that led to the 1215 Magna Carta, the peasants' revolt in 1381 through the poll tax riots in 1990 and the decision by lorry drivers to bring the country to a halt in 2000 in protest at the rising tax on diesel. But perhaps the most famous tax rebellion was the Boston Tea Party when protests against taxation of tea on American colonists by the British parliament eventually led to the American revolutionary war and the creation of the United States of America.

> by raising or lowering tax rates, governments can influence how people and companies behave

Tax tools

By and large governments have five main options to raise tax revenue. These are taxes: on personal income; on personal wealth; in the form of contributions towards social security; on corporate income; and via indirect taxes such as VAT. As Figure 6.1 shows, income tax makes up a little over a third of the £592 billion the UK government expected to raise in the year to April 2013 while VAT made up around a sixth.

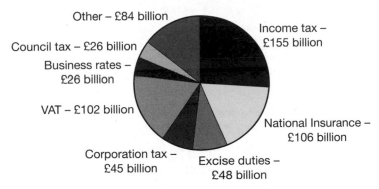

Figure 6.1 Sources of government revenue, 2012/13

Note: Office for Budget Responsibility, 2012-13 estimates. Other receipts include capital taxes, stamp duties, vehicle excise duties and some other tax and non-tax receipts – for example, interest and dividends. Figures may not sum due to rounding.

Source: Executive Summary, Budget 2012, chart 2, p. 7, http://cdn.hm-treasury.gov.uk/ budget2012_executive_summary.pdf

Taxes on personal income are the easiest to understand. Someone who works pays a certain share of his or her income in tax. For many employees the relative simplicity of the tax system means that their employers take the tax element out of their pay packet and send it to the government. This means they receive their monthly or weekly pay packet net of tax and do not need to worry about declaring the income to the taxman.

However, there are some features that complicate the picture. Countries such as the UK exclude the first chunk of income from any tax. This means that people who earn very little do not get caught up in the tax system. Many countries then have different rates of tax that get larger as people's income goes up. This is known as a 'progressive' system as it means that those who earn more pay proportionately more of their income in tax. A 'regressive' system is where the tax takes a larger percentage from low-income people than from high-income people. Currently the UK has three rates of income tax – 20%, 40% and 45%, for the highest earners.

The tax rates and the thresholds at which people move from one band to another can affect how they behave in two main ways. Firstly, changes in tax rates will affect their desire to work rather than stay at home. However, exactly how that works is unclear. One theory says that a higher tax rate reduces the reward for working. This means individuals have an incentive to work less and take more leisure time. This is known as the substitution effect.

Alternatively workers will realise that the higher tax rate means they will have lower take-home pay unless they work longer. This is known as the income effect. The other main impact is to encourage people to leave the workforce, for example by emigrating or retiring. It is difficult to predict how people will respond to changes in taxes. Arthur Laffer, an American economist, said there was an optimal level above which higher taxes would not raise extra revenue for the government as people reduced their production or found ways to avoid the tax. The graph that summarises his findings is known as the Laffer curve.

 **brilliant** example

Marginal tax rate

Back in the 1970s the UK had a top tax rate of 83% for five years, which meant that above a certain level of income, of every extra pound that someone earned 83p went to the taxman and just 17p was kept by the worker. An investment income surcharge raised the top rate on investment income to 98%, the highest permanent rate since the war. This applied to incomes over £20,000 (£170,500 in 2013 prices). The Labour Chancellor at the time, Denis Healey, was reputed to have said he would 'tax the rich until the pips squeak', although he always denied saying that. More recently, in 2012 the incoming French government announced a top rate of tax of 75%. This led to many famous wealthy French people announcing they were moving to a different country to escape paying the higher rate. What people don't realise is that in neither case will people have to pay the highest rate on all their income but only on the last chunk of money that they earn.

People in work also make a contribution to their future pension plans. In the UK this is known as National Insurance and in the US as 401k, but in both cases they are deducted from salaries. People may also have to pay taxes on the profits that they make by owning assets. Most assets are liable to Capital Gains Tax when you sell or dispose of them. These include shares, property, business assets and personal possessions. In the UK some assets are exempt – such as someone's car and, in most cases, their main home. Many governments impose a tax on assets that are passed down through a will after the owner dies (known as inheritance taxes or colloquially as 'death duties').

Businesses pay tax, although as a company is not a person the burden of the tax they pay must be borne by shareholders (which means they receive a lower share of profits), employees (who will receive reduced wages) or customers (who will pay higher prices). Businesses are liable for tax on their profits. This is why news reports about companies' annual financial results often use 'pre-tax profit' as the measure of how well they have done. Employers may also be required to pay social security contributions for their staff. In addition, different countries impose a range of taxes on the property businesses own and some of their activities such as those causing pollution.

 **brilliant** example

Global companies

At the end of 2012 a number of major global companies, including coffee retailer Starbucks, online retailer Amazon and internet search engine Google, came under fire for paying very low amounts of tax on their UK profits. While the companies were taking advantage of opportunities offered to reduce their tax payments, it led to anger among politicians and protests by members of the public who accused the companies of avoiding their moral duty. For some people it is a sign that the tax system is too complicated.

Indirect taxes are taxes that are paid when people spend money rather than when they earn it. The most common is a sales tax, known as VAT in many European countries or sales tax in the US. When someone goes to a shop, some of the money that they hand to the cashier to buy their goods – currently 20% in the UK – is forwarded by the retailer to the government, which is why it is known as an indirect tax. Government impose higher taxes on activities that they want to discourage. Alcoholic drinks and cigarettes carry an excise duty on top of VAT. However, some items such as children's clothes are not liable for VAT. Motorists too pay a further tax that is meant to cover the costs that they impose on the environment. While home-ownership is not something governments seek to discourage, all homebuyers in the UK have to pay the Stamp Duty Land Tax when they buy a property.

Keep it simple

Tax legislation has grown exponentially in recent years. As governments find more ways of taxing people and as companies and individuals find new ways to avoid tax, politicians are forced to draw up new rules, so the number of tax laws has increased. In 2009 it was calculated that the UK's tax code had more than doubled in size since 1997, going from 4,998 pages to 11,520.

> tax legislation has grown exponentially in recent years

In *The Wealth of Nations*, economist Adam Smith set out the four basic principles that he saw as essential to building a good tax system. He called them the 'Original or Main Canons of Taxation'. They are:

1 **Equity**. Tax payments should be proportional to income.
2 **Certainty**. Tax liabilities should be clear and certain.
3 **Convenience**. Taxes should be collected at a time and in a manner convenient for the taxpayer.
4 **Economy**. Taxes should not be expensive to collect and should not discourage business.

But over time economists have felt the need to add other canons to adapt to changing times:

1 **Productivity**. The methods of collecting taxes should not affect the productive activities of the state in a way that does not promote growth.

2 **Elasticity**. When the needs of the state increase, the revenue of the government also simultaneously increases in order to finance various projects and schemes.

3 **Simplicity**. The tax system should be simple to use so that taxpayers know how much they owe and to reduce the opportunity for corruption.

4 **Diversity**. The government should collect taxes from different sources rather than concentrating on a single source of tax.

Government spending

The other side of the balance sheet is government expenditure. While there are large variations in the amount that different countries' governments spend there are some categories that most share. The common area for expenditure is focused on services that it is not possible for individuals to organise but which benefit everyone equally. These include military defence, emergency services, criminal justice such as the police and fire service and street lighting. The rest of the budget is taken up with services that people could pay for themselves but which the government believes for public policy reasons are best provided centrally and funded, at least in part, by taxes. In this group often fall health services, education and social security or unemployment payments. Figure 6.2 shows the breakdown of the £683 billion spending according to the main UK government departments in the year to April 2013.

> how much money the government spends on one activity compared to another is a political decision

How much money the government spends on one activity compared to another is a political decision as it determines how much of a role the state plays in people's lives, from the amount of money given in benefits to those out of work to the amount spent on the military.

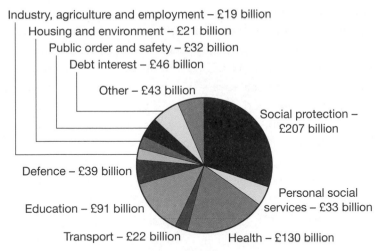

Industry, agriculture and employment – £19 billion
Housing and environment – £21 billion
Public order and safety – £32 billion
Debt interest – £46 billion
Other – £43 billion
Social protection –
£207 billion
Defence – £39 billion
Personal social
services – £33 billion
Education – £91 billion
Transport – £22 billion   Health – £130 billion

Figure 6.2 Spending of the main UK government departments, 2012/13
Note: Office for Budget Responsibility, 2012-13 estimates. Allocations to functions are based on HM Treasury analyses.
Source: Executive Summary, Budget 2012, chart 1, p.6, http://cdn.hm-treasury.gov.uk/ budget2012_executive_summary.pdf

Balancing the books

Like all households and corporations, governments have to plan how much money they are going to spend and how much they hope to receive. Most governments announce their figures for the latest year and unveil their forecasts for future years. In the UK, this happens at the Budget, an announcement to Parliament which is usually held in the spring.

While these budget books can extend to hundreds of pages, there are a few figures that can reveal what is going on. In any year the government will raise a certain amount in tax revenue and can show how much it spent. If those two figures are the same then the country has a balanced budget. If taxes are higher than spending its budget is in surplus and if spending is outstripping tax revenues then it has a budget deficit. This is often called the total or fiscal surplus or deficit.

In order to see how well the government is doing in a particular year you need to remove the interest payments on government debt that has been built up as a result of past deficits. Tax revenue minus spending minus interest payments is known as the primary budget balance. This distinction is often useful in seeing how countries that have been through a major debt crisis are performing on a year-by-year basis, ignoring the effect on the debt burden they are carrying.

brilliant explanation

Deficit and debt

People often use these terms interchangeably as meaning the amount the government owes. In fact they are very different. The deficit is the difference between the tax and spending in any one year. This debt is the total of all the deficits chalked up each year. If the government makes a surplus, then that money can be used to pay off some of the debt. Economists refer to this as the difference between a 'flow' (the deficit) and a 'stock' (the debt). A good analogy is a credit card. Each month you are told how much you owe – your deficit. You can pay it off and return to zero or you can keep it on the card and it becomes your debt. Each month the debt will increase by the amount you have spent and the amount of interest charged.

The public finances are also affected by the business cycles we saw in Chapter 3. During a downturn tax revenues usually fall as economic activity slows while social security payments rise as people lose their jobs. This is known as automatic fiscal policy or automatic stabilisers as these changes happen without any change in government policy. Economists calculate how much of the primary deficit or surplus is due to the cycle and can be expected to disappear as the economy returns to trend. This element is known as the cyclical budget and the rest is the structural budget, which will stay even after the economy returns to trend. The structural budget is also known as the cyclically adjusted budget.

One term that arises in the wake of a crisis in a country's public finances is 'primary surplus'. Simply this is the amount by which a government's total expenditure exceeds its total revenue, excluding interest payments on its debt. This is important because a highly indebted country will have to make high interest payments. Only by stripping those out can you see if the country is now spending less than it is raising in tax and so reducing the debt. In other words, it provides an indicator of current fiscal effort, since interest payments are predetermined by the size of previous deficits.

Governments that run deficits and debts need to borrow money to balance their books. They do this by issuing government bonds, known in the US as Treasury bonds or notes and in the UK as gilts. These are effectively IOUs from the government to investors with a commitment to pay interest to the lender. The amount that a government needs to borrow is its borrowing requirement. This is often expressed as a percentage of GDP – i.e. how much the government is borrowing compared to its annual economic output. A book looking at financial crises going back over eight centuries, *This Time is Different*, by Carmen Reinhart and Kenneth Rogoff found that for emerging market countries the risk of a crisis occurring rose when the figure rose above 30%.

brilliant quotation

'I used to think if there was reincarnation, I wanted to come back as the president or the pope. But now I want to come back as the bond market. You can intimidate everybody.'

James Carville, US presidential election campaign manager, 1993

While the government sets the duration of the loan and the interest rate, bonds find their own prices and interest rates in the open market. The interest rate that government has to pay will depend in part on how long it wants to borrow for. Bonds issued for 10 years will usually require a higher interest rate than one-year bonds to compensate investors for tying up their money for an extra nine years. However, it will also depend on other economic factors such as how well the country's economy is performing and how worried investors are that the country might default on its debt.

 **example**

Negative yield curves

The European debt crisis led to a number of countries such as Greece, Portugal and Ireland defaulting on their debts and going through a bailout process that saw bondholders – people who had loaned their governments money – lose money. Investors that needed to invest in European government debt rushed to buy German bonds, which were seen as some of the safest investments in those volatile times. The demand was so high that in July 2012 Germany was able to sell €4.2 billion of two-year bonds at an average yield of minus 0.06%. This means it will pay back less money in two years to investors than it received. The country also did not need to offer any interest payments.

The investors who lend money to governments by buying their bonds can then buy and sell bonds between each other. This means that government bonds can find their own price level in the market. The interest rate on a bond is also known as the yield. This is calculated relative to the price of the bond, which means that the price and yield move in opposite directions. If a bond of £100,000 pays £2,000 a year then its yield is 2%. If the country gets into trouble and the bond price falls to

£50,000 then the yield becomes 4%. The yield is therefore a useful measure of how much faith the financial markets have in a government. The yield will be seen as the interest rate the country would have to offer to borrow more money and avoid a

> yield is a useful measure of how much faith the financial markets have in a government

default. During the recent eurozone debt crisis many analysts saw a yield of government debt above 6% as a sign that the country was in danger of default.

 **brilliant** explanation

Credit rating agencies

Another measure of how much confidence the financial markets have in the state of a government's finances is given by the credit ratings agencies. These are private companies whose job it is to assess a country – they also analyse companies and individual projects and loans – and decide how likely it is that they will default on their debt. There are nine major ratings agencies but the three that we hear most about are Standard & Poor's, Fitch ratings and Moody's. They assign a grade ranging from AAA, known colloquially as triple-A, which indicates there is almost no chance of default, down to D, which indicates the country has gone bust.

The role of fiscal policy

As well as allowing the automatic stabilisers to operate, governments can use their tax and spending powers to alter the way that the economy runs. This may be because of a specific public policy goal, such as deciding to build a new road to a town in the expectation that the better transport connections will lead to job and wealth creation. It could be driven by the need to offset a major economic downturn. We saw in

Chapter 2 that one of the big dividing lines between classical and Keynesian economics was over whether the public sector should intervene in the running of the economy or stay out and leave the private sector to sort out any problems.

This has become one of the key dividing lines between politicians on both sides of the Atlantic. The European Union and a number of large member countries such as the UK and Germany believe that the main priority should be to reduce the deficit and lower the debt burden. In order to achieve this they announced a range of spending cuts and tax rises for their own countries and for crisis-hit countries such as Greece and Ireland – commonly known as austerity measures. However, modern Keynesian economists believe that the government needs to step in and support economic growth at a time when households are cutting spending to try to reduce their own debts – even at the cost of higher deficits in the short run. Advocates of austerity point to Ireland's success in reducing its deficit. Critics point to the US, which implemented stimulus measures and whose economy in 2013 was above the level before the crisis, in contrast with many European countries whose economies are smaller than they were in 2007.

Whatever the rights and wrongs of the argument, it is worth remembering what happens when the government raises and decreases the amount it spends, and increases or lowers taxes. In theory increases in government expenditure will increase overall economic activity (what economists call aggregate demand) by putting more money into the economic system.

Multiplication test

One major and controversial issue is how much aggregate demand extra government spending will create. In the case of a new road, while the cost to the government may be £1 million, the work it will bring to companies down the supply chain may lead to extra demand as firms feel confident enough to take on new workers and households feel more confident to spend as a result of the new employment. This is known as the fiscal multiplier. If the government believes that the £1 million project will lead to a total boost to output of £1.5 million then the multiplier is 1.5.

The multiplier can be less than 1, which would indicate that the boost to economic growth is actually less than the amount of money pumped in. In October 2012 the International Monetary Fund (the global financial watchdog that was set up in 1944 to monitor the global economy) said that it had used a multiplier estimate of 0.5 to produce its recent economic forecasts. But it now believed that the multipliers had actually been in the 0.9 to 1.7 range since the Great Recession. Multipliers also apply when governments cut spending, as many have done to balance their budgets in the wake of the crisis. In this case a multiplier larger than 1 would indicate that the cut in government spending has cut economic output by a greater amount than it has contributed.

One reason why some economists believe that fiscal multipliers do not boost economic activity is because they believe that businesses and households react to policy decisions. One criticism is that extra government spending 'crowds out' private sector spending. It does this, they say, by forcing interest rates up to levels at which private firms cannot borrow. Also by hiring staff and buying in equipment and supplies, they force companies to pay more to compete with the government for staff, goods and services. A final argument is that the government is likely to carry out the work less efficiently than the private sector would have done.

Another critique was set out by David Ricardo, a British economist and MP, in the 19th century. He said that when the government borrows, consumers and companies in the private sector anticipate that taxes will have to rise in the future and so build up their own savings. This in effect counteracts the stimulus that would otherwise come from the extra borrowing. His idea is known as Ricardian equivalence. Naturally Keynesians disagree: Nobel laureate Paul Krugman has said that it only makes sense 'if consumers have perfect foresight, live forever, and have perfect access to capital markets'.

 brilliant recap

- The government is a major player in most countries' economies.
- The public influences growth through taxation and spending.
- The main taxes are on income, wealth, company profits and on spending.
- Governments spend money on activities that either cannot be done by private individuals or which it feels should be done centrally.
- Annual budgets show whether taxes and spending are in balance.
- Governments with a deficit have to borrow money.
- Borrowing tends to go up during recessions and down during booms.
- There is a debate over whether the government should borrow to boost economic growth.

CHAPTER 7

Interest rates, monetary policy and central banks

'The most powerful force in the universe is compound interest.'

Albert Einstein, scientist (attributed), 1879–1955

They say that everything has its price and that is true even for money. Interest rates are the price of money – although strictly speaking interest rates are more accurately the price for borrowing or lending money. Anyone who has a mortgage, or has taken out a loan with their bank to fund their business or pay for a holiday knows that interest rates matter. Equally, anyone who has tucked their nest egg away in a savings account will know that the interest rate is one of the most important parts of the deal.

Just as the price of a good or service will affect how much demand and supply there is, so interest rates will influence how keen people and businesses are to save or borrow. Consumers will use or read about many different types of interest rates. As well as different rates for lending and borrowing there are long-term and short-term interest rates. The interest can also be fixed for a certain period or it can rise and fall in line with market conditions. All these factors can be decided on by the lender and borrower and will determine the final cost to the borrower. If interest rates are low people

> interest rates will help determine the demand and supply of money

will be less keen to lock their money away as it will earn relatively little. Equally they might be happier to borrow because they will have to pay the lender less. Interest rates will therefore help determine the demand and supply of money, which in turn will influence economic activity and inflation.

Which interest rate?

When journalists talk about interest rates, they almost always mean the interest rate set by the central bank. But that rate is seldom the one that ordinary borrowers pay or savers receive. For many years since the global financial crisis, official interest rates in the UK, eurozone, Japan and the United States have been close to zero – yet no one can borrow money at those rates.

At the end of the day, the interest rates that people pay will be different from the rate that the central bank sets, even if the level of the official rate has a major influence on how other interest rates are set. While the central bank will effectively set a floor on rates, there are a number of factors that determine what rates savers and borrowers will earn or pay on the many different products that are available. You only have to look at the interest that you earn on your bank account and the payments on your mortgage to see the range.

One factor influencing the rate is the length of time you are borrowing or saving for. People who lend money for a long time – whether a bank issuing a mortgage or an individual tying up their money in a fixed-term savings account – are losing the ability to do anything else with that money in the meantime. The longer the term of the loan the higher the interest rate is likely to be.

Another factor is the risk involved. A government bond is seen as very low risk because the state will always be able to raise taxes to pay off its debts. The interest rate – or yield as it is known in financial markets – tends to be low. Recently some governments in the eurozone have come close to defaulting on their debts. Because of the higher risk that investors won't get their money back, the yields have risen to very high levels. Interest rates on credit cards and loans for major purchases such as cars and furniture are also likely to price in a risk that the borrower will default on the loan.

Inflation will also affect interest rate levels as the higher the inflation rate the more interest rates are likely to rise. As inflation erodes the spending power of money, lenders will want to charge a higher interest rate to offset the decrease in the purchasing power of the money they will be repaid at the end of the loan.

brilliant fact

LIBOR

One factor that determines interest rates in the market is the rate at which banks lend to each other, known as LIBOR or London interbank offer rate. The sterling three-month LIBOR rate influences the level at which lenders set key rates on mortgages to consumers and on loans to businesses. As it is the rate at which banks are happy to lend to each other during the credit crunch it became known as a measure of how much they trusted each other. However, in 2011 it emerged that traders within some banks had been understating the borrowing costs they reported for LIBOR. Some banks have faced criminal sanctions and regulators are looking at reforming the way the rate is set.

If a loan or savings product has a variable interest rate, then that rate will rise or fall as the central bank moves rates. The alternative is to agree on a fixed rate, which means that the interest rate a customer receives or pays will not change over the duration of the loan or investment. This can protect against inflation. If a homeowner has taken out a mortgage at 5%, the payments will stay the same even if the central bank raises interest rates sharply. Of course a saver who has a fixed rate account will see the value of their interest payments stay the same if bank rates change. If the central bank is raising rates to fight rising inflation, then the saver will be worse off as the value of the interest payments will be eroded by inflation. This means that borrowers and lenders are effectively taking a bet on the path of interest rates and inflation when they agree on a rate.

Compound interest

There is an urban myth that Albert Einstein referred to compound interest as the most powerful force in the universe. Whether he truly said that, it is clear that compound interest is something that both savers and borrowers should be aware of. Simply put, the idea is that a saver with an interest-bearing account who adds the income to the original sum saved will next year be paid interest on the original capital plus the first year's interest.

It is worth remembering that debt interest works the same way but in reverse if the repayments are not made. If the payment is not met, the interest gets added to the principal, which leads to a higher interest payment next time. This is effectively negative compound interest as it makes the borrower poorer.

---

brilliant explanation

Compound interest works like magic when money is left earning interest for some time. If we take £1,000 invested at 10% with each year's income added to the principal, after a year it would be worth £1,100. The following year the 10% would apply to the £1,100 and would grow to £1,210 and after five years will be worth £1,610. A handy rule of thumb is the idea that a saver can divide the interest rates they are receiving into 72 to see how long it will take to double their original investment. So £1 invested at 10% would take 7.2 years ((72/10) = 7.2) to turn into £2.

It is important to understand exactly what the interest rate means. Most people would understand a 5% annual interest rate to mean that they would pay £50 to borrow £1,000 over one year. This calculation – taking the annual interest charged, dividing it by the total loan amount and then multiplying by 100 – is known as the annual percentage rate (APR). An effective APR or EAR (effective annual interest rate) takes into account the impact of interest on any fees for the loans and the impact of compound interest if payments are charged monthly, for example.

brilliant example

Short-term loans for people who need cash in a hurry – known as payday loans – often have interest rates that seem eye-wateringly high. Lenders charge a fee for the loan usually expressed as a flat fee per £100 borrowed for the stated short period – until payday. Although they are designed to be taken out for short periods the lenders have to publish annual APRs, which can end up at more than 4,000%. Lenders say APRs are an inappropriate measure, as they are distorted by the short length of the loans and are not designed to be taken out for a full year.

Setting the rate

So how do central banks set their interest rate – and why is that rate so important when no one borrows or saves at that price? The reason is that interest rates can act as a brake or an accelerator on economic growth and inflation. The ability to influence interest rates becomes a very important tool for policymakers trying to ensure stable economic growth without too much inflation. In many countries the power to set short-term interest

> interest rates can act as a brake or an accelerator on economic growth and inflation

rates rests with the central bank. The Bank of England sets interest rates for the UK while the other main central banks include the US Federal Reserve, the European Central Bank, the Bank of Japan and the Swiss National Bank.

While they only set one or sometimes two interest rates, this gives central banks the power to influence the interest rates across the economy. The central bank sets the interest rate at which financial institutions, such as banks and building societies, must borrow money.

A central bank has the power to move interest rates because it is the monopoly supplier of 'base money' - the notes and coins in circulation and the deposits commercial banks must keep on reserve with it. Banks that supply banknotes for their customers, either over the counter or through automatic teller machines, obtain them from the central bank. Banks also need to borrow money overnight to ensure they meet those reserve requirements. Any change in the official rate is passed on very quickly to private banks, building societies and other financial institutions when they lend to other banks. In turn this influences the cost of borrowing and saving and interest rates set by banks and other lenders for products such as mortgages and overdrafts. It may also affect the price of financial assets, such as bonds and shares, and the exchange rate, which affects consumer and business demand in a variety of ways.

brilliant quotation

One of the catchiest ways of explaining how central banks work is attributed to William McChesney Martin, who was chairman of the US Federal Reserve for almost 20 years up to 1970. 'I'm the fellow who takes away the punch bowl just when the party is getting good', he said, to explain why the central bank had to raise interest rates.

Transmission mechanism

The way in which the central bank can influence the economy with exchange rates is known as the 'transmission mechanism'.

There are four main channels through which a change in interest rates feeds through to the wider economy. These are:

- The way it leads private sector financial institutions to change the rates they charge for overdrafts, loans and mortgages and which they offer to savers. While some rates will change immediately, others, such as fixed rate loans, will only change when new products are offered. But the net effect is to change the rate at which consumers and businesses save and borrow.

- The impact on asset prices such as homes and shares. A cut in interest rates will lead to lower mortgage rates, which will make it easier to borrow to buy a house. As demand for property rises this is likely to lead to a rise in house prices. As homeowners see the value of their wealth rise, they are more likely to spend. Higher house prices enable existing homeowners to extend their mortgages in order to finance higher consumption. Share prices rise as traders expect the higher economic activity that follows drops in interest rates to boost company profits. Higher share prices raise households' wealth and can increase their willingness to spend, either because they own shares or because they get lifted by a tide of optimism.

- Changes in interest rates can also alter people's expectations about the future path for the economy and for inflation. It also affects people's confidence in the outlook both for the economy and for their own finances. Both expectations and confidence will affect how people behave. However, this is not always easy to predict. For instance, a hike in interest rates could be seen as a sign that the central bank believes the economy is likely to grow faster than previously thought, giving a boost to expectations of future growth and confidence in general. However, it is also possible that it would be interpreted as a signal that the bank sees the need to slow the growth in the economy in order to hit the inflation target, and this could dent expectations of future growth and lower confidence.

- The exchange rate. A cut in interest rates could lead investors to move their money to other economies where interest rates have not changed, causing the exchange rate to weaken. This in turn would make imports more expensive for domestic firms but would make their exports cheaper for foreign buyers. A rate hike might have the opposite effect but in both cases there would be effects on growth and inflation.

 brilliant history

The Bank of England still has a weather vane in its Court Room, which tells the Bank's directors which way the wind is blowing. A couple of centuries ago one of the main drivers of the demand for credit was the direction of the wind, which indicated when conditions were favourable for ships to enter or leave the port of London and so whether more credit needed to be made available.

Given the many different channels of transmission and the uncertainty over how different actors will respond, the impact of a rate change will not be felt overnight. The Bank of England, for example, believes that it takes up to a year for the full effect on output to happen. The maximum impact of a change in rates on inflation takes up to two years.

How a central bank works

Given the importance of interest rates for growth and inflation, it is worth looking at what these central banks are and how they go about their job. Central banks are the arm of a country's government that runs its monetary policy, which includes managing the money supply as well as setting interest rates, and looks after financial stability. In some countries it also supervises the private banking sector, acts as the government's banker and looks after its gold reserves. Increasingly central banks are separate from the political process and are run by professional economists and financiers rather than elected politicians.

Given the two-year lag between decisions on interest rates and their effect on inflation, central banks have to take decisions on monetary policy based on judgements about what inflation might be – the outlook over the coming few years – not what it is now. To do this they use models of the economy to forecast inflation based on a range of factors such as money and asset prices, demand by consumers and businesses, likely output and supply, and future costs and prices. These are then used to predict the medium term prospects for inflation and the risks to that outlook.

> increasingly central banks are separate from the political process

Most central banks review the interest rate that they set once a month or thereabouts. Either the Governor on his or her own or together with a group of fellow bank officials and sometimes outside experts, announces whether the rate has stayed the same or changed, either up or down. This is a huge event for the financial markets and a lot of economists spend considerable time trying to second-guess what the major banks will do. All speeches, comments and interviews given by those with the power to set interest rates are pored over for clues to the next move. Some banks, such as the Swedish Riksbank – which is the oldest remaining central bank in the world, founded in 1668 – even set out how they expect to change their own interest rate over the coming couple of years.

Monetary policy and picking targets

While most of today's central banks now primarily target inflation, that move is a relatively recent development. Monetary policy can have a number of goals. They include stimulating economic growth, keeping unemployment low, ensuring financial stability, targeting the money supply or aiming for a certain exchange rate. These goals can often run against each other. For example, raising interest rates to lower inflation will run the risk of slowing economic growth and of triggering a fall in the exchange rate.

After the Second World War many governments used fiscal policy – government spending and taxation – to stimulate the economy or slow it down. However, after the oil shocks of the 1970s saw a spike in inflation, government decided that use of monetary policies were needed to bring inflation back down. Initially many targeted the money supply or the value of the currency in relation to another currency. However over time central banks realised that the relationship between growth in the money supply and the performance of the economy was not as strong as they had thought and they stopped targeting the money supply. Countries that pegged their currency to another country sometimes constrained the central bank's ability to respond to such shocks. The UK found this when it had to leave the European exchange rate mechanism in 1992.

> many central banks adopted inflation targeting

Inflation targets

Many central banks adopted inflation targeting as a pragmatic response to the failure of those other monetary policy regimes. Inflation targeting was pioneered by the Reserve Bank New Zealand, which in December 1989 became the first central bank to set a specific target band for inflation. This style of inflation targeting is now shared with a number of major economies including the UK, Canada, Norway, Poland, South Africa, Sweden and Australia. The eurozone, where the European Central Bank runs monetary policy for the 17 member countries (as of early 2013) of the euro, also has a numerical target but has other more general goals as well. Non-inflation targeters include the US Federal Reserve, which is responsible for monetary policy in the world's largest economy and is tasked with 'promoting effectively' the goals of maximum employment, stable prices and moderate long-term interest rates. The objective of the People's Bank of China is to 'maintain the stability of the value of the currency and thereby promote economic growth'.

Economists say that a number of things must be put in place to make a success of targeting inflation. The central bank can conduct monetary policy with some degree of independence. The bank must not try to target other indicators, such as wages, the level of employment or the exchange rate. The bank or government should establish an explicit target for inflation over a specific time period. For example, the Bank of England is currently tasked to hit a target of 2% over two years. If inflation moves outside a range 1 percentage point on either side the Governor has to write a public letter of explanation to the Chancellor.

Using interest rates to target inflation has on the face of it been a success. Over the last decade consumer price inflation has been low and stable in most major economies. Part of the reason for the success is that central banks have succeeded in convincing consumers and businesses that they are serious about hitting their target, which is most frequently 2%. This creates a virtuous circle as businesses and workers then tend to make decisions over pay rises and price hikes in the knowledge that a rise in inflation as a result is likely to be met by a rise in interest rates. Central banks can then look at surveys of people's inflation expectations to gauge whether people are expecting inflation to rise.

However, at the same time, many countries have experienced episodes – indeed some severe episodes if we include the financial crisis of 2007/08 – of monetary instability in many guises, including asset price instability, financial system instability, and exchange rate crises.

There is an argument that by focusing solely on inflation, central banks ignored asset price bubbles and other changes in the financial system in the first decade of this century that ultimately led to the Great Recession. It had been assumed that this inflation-fighting mandate would automatically lead to financial stability and that the framework of monetary policy could deal with cross-border capital flows. There is now a live debate over whether central banks should target other indicators instead of or as well as inflation, including asset prices and economic output in the form of nominal GDP (total economic activity before taking inflation into account).

Quantitative easing

The financial crisis forced the major central banks of the world to respond by cutting interest rates to close to zero. As interest rates cannot fall below zero, these banks decided to increase the money supply by buying government securities or other securities from the market. This mechanism, which is known by the technical term of quantitative easing or QE, increases the money supply by flooding financial institutions with capital in a bid to encourage increased lending and provide extra liquidity.

Although no actual new banknotes are printed, QE has the same effect as printing notes by creating electronic money on institutions' balance sheets. QE electronically creates new money and uses it to buy government bonds from private investors such as pension funds and insurance companies. These investors typically do not want to hold on to this money, because it yields a low return. So they tend to use it to purchase other assets, such as corporate bonds and shares. That lowers longer-term borrowing costs and encourages the issuance of new equities and bonds.

The risk with this policy is that because it involves injecting new money into the economy, it will eventually lead to a rise in inflation as more money is chasing the same amount of goods and services. However, this risk will fade if the policy works and the economy starts to grow rapidly again. In any event central banks that have implemented QE have said that they are ready to withdraw the stimulus if inflation starts to rise. The other risk is that the financial institutions that benefit from QE use the money to bolster their own finances or to pay dividends to shareholders and higher rewards to employees rather than increasing lending to small businesses and consumers.

> QE electronically creates new money and uses it to buy government bonds

However, some economists fear that pushing interest rates close to zero and injecting huge amounts of cash into the system will create what Keynes called a 'liquidity trap'. This happens when consumers decide to hoard cash rather than spend it for fear of another crisis or a move to deflation.

Nominal GDP: a new target?

One legacy from the financial crisis has been a debate over whether an inflation target is the best way to run monetary policy. While the Bank of England and other central banks succeeded in bringing inflation down in the two decades since 1992, there are concerns that their strict adherence to fighting inflation meant they failed to see the build-up of pressures elsewhere in the financial system. These pressures formed the basis for the outbreak of the crisis and these countries have struggled to stimulate a substantial recovery while inflation has stayed above target.

Veteran economists such as Samuel Brittan of the *Financial Times* have for some time argued for central banks to target nominal GDP – i.e. the actual cash value of the growth in the economy that does not take inflation into account. This would mean that the Bank would now become responsible for hitting a particular level of economic growth rather than inflation. Mark Carney, the Canadian central banker who took over as Governor of the Bank of England in June 2013, has discussed the idea as a way of stimulating the economy. UK Chancellor George Osborne wants academics, who have debated the idea for years, to lead a debate.

For example, if we set a nominal GDP target of 4.5% we might hope that inflation would be close to the current target of 2% in the UK while the rest would be real post-inflation economic growth. But of course with one target you can't choose how it is achieved. Unlike inflation, where the target is always forward looking, achieving the nominal growth, this target would involve ensuring that periods of low growth were made up for with periods of faster growth – perhaps by setting interest rates to stimulate activity. As Dr Carney said in December 2012: 'Bygones are not bygones.'

Another approach would be to target unemployment. The US Fed has always had unemployment in its mandate but in December 2012 Chairman Ben Bernanke announced that the Fed would keep interest rates close to zero until unemployment fell below 6.5% and as long as its inflation forecast stays below 2.5%.

brilliant fact

Why nominal GDP is a good target	Why it is worse than inflation target
Bank responsible for economic growth	Could open the door to inflation
Cannot just forget poor past growth	GDP data comes out with a delay
More room for Bank to stimulate growth	GDP data can be revised
Easier to respond to one-off shocks	People don't understand nominal GDP

brilliant recap

- The interest rate is the price in % of borrowing money for a year.
- It is charged when the money is being borrowed, and paid when it is being loaned.
- Interest rates can be found on credit cards, overdrafts and savings accounts.
- They have become the main tool for central banks to fight inflation.
- Raising interest rates will bring down inflation but slow growth.
- Cutting rates should encourage growth but may fuel inflation.
- When interest rates fall close to zero central banks have to inject money into the economy – this is known as quantitative easing.

CHAPTER 8

Money and finance

'All I ask is the chance to prove that money can't make me happy.'

Spike Milligan, comedian and actor (1918–2002)

Money is the lifeblood of an economy. The love of money may be the root of all evil, as the famous verse from the Bible says, but for a lot of people money – and particularly the lack of it – is the cause of many of their worries. Despite its importance, when people reach into their wallet or purse for a note or coins, few will ponder on how it is that a lump of nickel-brass or a piece of fabric allows them to buy a pint of milk, newspaper or cup of coffee.

Just as money is important to households in their everyday life, it is also an essential concept for economists in their struggle to understand how the economy works. Money exists not just as notes and coins but also increasingly in many different forms that are used by both households and businesses. But to understand how they fit together and

> for a lot of people money is the cause of many of their worries

how the ability to borrow money was a key ingredient in the 2008 financial crisis, we first have to go back to ancient history.

From cows to coins

Back in the mists of time there are records of people engaging in barter – exchanging goods such as cows and grain for goods of similar value. However this was cumbersome and highly inefficient. A farmer with wheat who wanted to buy some sheep would have to find a shepherd who wanted to buy grain. Economists call this unlikely combination 'the dual coincidence of wants'.

The drawbacks of this system meant that civilisations quickly moved on to using commodities such as gold and silver that can be made into coins, but also foods and commodities. The Roman rulers paid their soldiers partly in salt, a fact that gives us the word salary (from the Latin *salis* for salt) and the phrase that a worker is 'worth their salt'. This was known as commodity money as its value is linked to the value of the item.

However it was cumbersome and risky to carry around large quantities of precious metal coins. So the final step was the issue of 'promissory notes' by people holding gold or silver, promising to pay the bearer the value printed or written on it. Over time, money has moved from something that can be converted to a physical asset to an agreement between governments and citizens. Technically, this is known as 'fiat' currency from the Latin for 'let it be'. Up until 1971 when the leading countries ended gold convertibility, it was possible to present a coin or note to a bank and ask for a certain amount of gold or another physical asset in return.

Technically money must serve three key purposes, according to economists. These factors, which also broadly contribute to the demand for money, are:

- A unit of account such as sterling, the US dollar, Japanese yen and so on.
- A medium of exchange to facilitate trade in goods, services and financial instruments.
- A store of value that makes saving convenient.

The money in the economy is known as the money supply. The notes and coins printed and minted by the central bank is known as the 'monetary base' or as M0. The next category, M1, includes instant access bank accounts and the scale then goes up to M4 (in the UK; the US and rest of Europe use M3), which includes all money held by banks as well as claims against financial institutions and commercial paper and bonds with a maturity of up to five years. The higher the M-number the broader the scope and the less easy it is to turn back into cash – which economists call liquidity.

The important point here is while only the central bank can print money, banks can create credit through their lending activities. Banks can use the money that is held on deposit with them as a base to support their lending. They need to keep a certain amount of that – say 10% – in their coffers to ensure they can meet withdrawal requests. But they can lend out the remaining 90% to other customers who will spend the money. For example, a customer deposits £100 with their bank. The bank keeps £10 in reserve and lends £90 to another customer who spends that money in a shop. The shopkeeper deposits £90 in the bank, which can then take or use £81 out and keep £9 in reserve. As the money circulates through the economy it 'creates' more money on the banks' balance sheets. This works as long as all the depositors do not decide to try to withdraw their money at the same time!

brilliant history

Bank runs

In September 2007, TV news programmes in the UK were filled with images of queues going round the block from branches of Northern Rock, a bank that was strongly rumoured to be on the brink of bankruptcy after over-investing in long-term risky assets. Savers were desperate to withdraw their savings before the bank's assets were frozen. In one case, a couple barricaded a bank manager in her office after she refused to let them withdraw £1 million from their account. While shocking at the time, it was nothing new. In 1866 the Bank of England suspended payments to Overend, Gurney & Co., a bank that found itself in financial difficulties after making large investments in the railways. Crowds of savers from across the country gathered round its City of London headquarters.

Theories of money

Ensuring the correct amount of money is in circulation is one of the main jobs of central banks. If too little money is in circulation, households and businesses are likely to struggle to pay for daily expenses or get loans. Companies would be likely to go out of business, which, in turn, could increase unemployment. On the other hand, if there is too much money in circulation, loans could be readily available and people may spend more quickly and freely – potentially pushing up prices and leading to inflation.

The amount of money in the economy can have an impact on inflation, growth and financial stability although, as with so many economic issues, there are disagreements about how those connections work. The main dividing line is between monetarists and Keynesians.

The quantity theory of money, a key monetarist concept that we discussed in Chapter 1, says that changes in the money supply change the economy's price level but nothing else. It says that the quantity of money multiplied by the number of times the money is used must equal the volume of all goods and services sold multiplied by their price. The theory assumes that the volume of transactions and the number of times the money is used are not affected by an increase in the money supply. The net result therefore must be an increase in the price level. If the quantity of money in the economy doubles then the price of goods and services will on average double. This theory – or at least a modified version of it – led governments to try to control demand by targeting the money supply.

The Keynesian school disagrees with this. Its supporters argue that the price level is not strictly determined by the money supply. Instead the money supply influences the price level indirectly through its effects on interest rates, incomes, outputs, employment and investment. They also say that the theory breaks down in recessions, depressions or other times when the economy is not operating at full employment. The safest thing to say is that there is a link between money supply and inflation over the long run, but that the relationship in the short run is much weaker.

Household finance

Cash is very useful but most households could not manage their daily spending needs using notes and coins alone. Many families use a range of other ways of paying and borrowing – sometimes at the same time. People use cheques or debit cards, which take money straight out of their bank account. Other forms of payment build up a debt that needs to be paid off later. For small purchases these methods can include credit cards, store cards, hire purchase agreements and bank loans. Similarly, when it comes to making much larger purchases like a new home or a car, most people will need to be able to borrow money via a long-term loan. The ability to borrow is very useful as it enables people to buy a home, which would otherwise not be possible. Similarly, student loans enable people to borrow money in order to study and pay back the debt once they find a job.

However, too much debt can cause economic problems. Cumulatively these individual loans are known as household debt. According to the International Monetary Fund, the ratio of household debt to income rose by an average of 39 percentage points to 138% in the five years leading to 2007, the year that saw the start of the financial crisis. In some countries, such as Denmark, Iceland, Ireland, the Netherlands and Norway, debt peaked at more than 200% of household income. In other words, the total debt taken on by households was worth twice the amount they earned in a year. The IMF concluded that housing busts and recessions that were preceded by larger run-ups in household debt tended to be more severe and protracted.

In normal times households will pay off their debts from their income from wages and salaries and from investments. Many households will have assets, such as investments and their home, as well as debts. However, in an economic downturn they are more likely to lose their jobs or suffer a cut in wages. Meanwhile, the value of their savings and their property is also likely to fall. As a result households will try and reduce the amount of money they owe, by using savings to pay off the debt, reducing spending to leave more money for interest payments, waiting for the effect of inflation to reduce the value of the debt over time, negotiating with the lenders or applying for personal bankruptcy.

too much debt can cause economic problems

Many households also look to save some of their money by buying savings products and investments. During good economic times individuals are more willing to put their money into investments that produce greater rewards such as shares, property, commodities and more arcane investments such as art, stamps and wine. In a downturn they are likely to value safety more and so focus on cash and government bonds. Traders call this behaviour 'risk on and risk off'.

While many households put money in savings accounts and other investments they can access through their bank, they are also increasingly buying bonds and shares. Until 1986 UK investors who wanted to buy shares would go to a stockbroker who would go to the floor of the London Stock Exchange where people called 'jobbers' worked. The broker would buy shares from the jobber offering the lowest price and, in turn, sell them to the investor. After a change in the law known colloquially as the 'Big Bang', investors can now go directly through a broker. Computer technology means that people can buy and sell shares from home using an online stockbroker.

 **example**

Exchange traded products

Typically domestic investors will buy shares in companies based in their home country. However, an innovation allows them to buy into companies, stock markets and even commodities around the world. An exchange traded product (ETP) is a fund that tracks the performance of an underlying equity or bond index. The investor can buy or sell them just as they would a company share. As well as ETPs that track well-known indices such as the FTSE 100 share index, more unusual ETPs include ones that rise if a stock market falls and others that track commodities ranging from aluminium to zinc.

However, even in wealthy countries there are people with low levels of income and no assets. For these households the primary source of income will be social security payments from the government, which include payments to the unemployed, those unable to work due to illness or injury and pensioners, with extra payments for those who are caring for other family members. Some find it hard to open a bank account and have to go to organisations such as credit unions to borrow money. These

> even in wealthy countries there are people with low levels of income and no assets

are owned by their members and aim to provide access to low-cost loans. They also have a goal of helping people avoid unofficial lenders – often called 'loan sharks' – who regularly offer money at high rates of interest and threaten violence if they are not paid.

Financial markets

One of the most profound shifts in economics and finance in recent decades has been the opening up of the way that money can be moved around the world. Until the 1970s the systems for transferring money from one country to another were very laborious. Furthermore, many countries, including the UK right up to 1979, had capital controls that limited the amount of money that could be moved in and out of the country. For example, it was impossible – without using the black market – for Britons to take more than £50 with them when they went abroad.

Computer technology and internet communications have made it much easier to transfer money around the world. It is now possible for one trader to send billions of dollars with the push of a button. At the same time developed economies have decided that it is much better to allow inward investment and inflows of capital than it is to try and control them. The resulting ability to move money around the world is known as the liberalisation of capital markets.

The scale of the movements of money around the world is truly breath-taking. According to the Bank of International Settlements – an intergovernmental body that promotes discussion and collaboration among central banks – daily average foreign exchange market turnover reached $4 trillion in April 2010. In the US around $850 billion worth of bonds change hands every day. Meanwhile companies invested $1.6 trillion in overseas countries in 2012, according to the United Nations.

Complex finance and the sub-prime crisis

Since investors can now look around the world for places to put their money, this has led to the creation of a large number of new and highly complex financial products. We have come across stock markets and bond markets in *Brilliant Economics*, but these new arrivals come with their own language and a much higher degree of complexity. The growth in this world of complex financial instruments, such as the sub-prime mortgage securities described below, has been blamed for contributing to the 2007 financial crisis. One criticism was that the heads of the institutions that were buying these products did not understand what they consisted of and how they would behave if there were a major economic slowdown.

 **explanation**

The speed at which financial market euphoria turned into panic and despair in 2007/08 prompted economists to go back to an idea set out by the late American economics professor Hyman Minsky 15 years earlier. His financial instability hypothesis said that during booms, borrowing by companies and investors reaches a level at which they can no longer meet their payments from incoming revenues and are forced to sell their assets. This shift from stability to fragility to crisis is now known as a Minsky moment, although he did not use the phrase.

In the early years of the last decade low interest rates and inflation, rising financial markets and stable economic growth encouraged investors to look for investments that give greater returns. House prices had been rising quickly in many countries and there was a big rise in demand for mortgages. As prices continued to rise banks became more willing to lend to people with poor credit histories and modest incomes known as sub-prime mortgagees or NINJAs – No Income No Job or Assets.

In order to spread the risk the banks used a technique known as securitisation. The banks sold the mortgages to another finance house that would receive the regular payments from the mortgages. They then bundled up a package of mortgages and offered those as a security for investors to buy. These were known as mortgage-backed securities (MBS) but the same model was applied to commercial mortgages and business loans. These securities could then be mixed in with other tranches of loans and debts to create a collateralised debt obligation (CDO). Investors could buy CDOs that were themselves a mix of different CDOs. These were known as CDO squared – and even CDO cubed if the new packages are made up of CDO squareds.

House prices started falling in early 2007 after US interest rates rose from 1% to 5.35%. As borrowing costs soared it became clear that many sub-prime borrowers had taken on loans that they could not afford. Many took out adjustable rate mortgages with a fixed low rate for two years, after which the interest rate rose. As house prices fell and hundreds of thousands of mortgage-holders defaulted on their debt, the value of the complex financial products plummeted. Banks that were holding large amounts of these securities had to write off the losses. By early 2008 the IMF estimated the total write-downs at $510 billion with forecasts that the total impact would be $1–2 trillion.

The losses led a large number of banks in the US to fail, culminating in the collapse of Lehman Brothers investment bank in September 2008, which in turn caused the Great Recession of 2008/09. A number of banks in Europe had to be rescued, including Royal Bank of Scotland, Lloyds Banking Group and Northern Rock in the UK, as well as banks in France, Germany, Holland, Belgium and the Netherlands.

 **brilliant** explanation

Financial regulatory reform

In the wake of the crisis governments decided to embark on a major overhaul of the rules that governed financial institutions. The rules dictate how much money banks must hold in reserve against various forms of loans they make, with riskier loans attracting a higher reserve requirement. It also imposes rules aimed to ensure that banks have enough liquid cash available to survive a credit crunch of 30 days. The regime, which includes many other rules, is known as Basel III as it is the third version of regulations originally set down by a committee of bankers in the Swiss city of Basel in 1992. The international banking industry has claimed that full implementation will cut economic growth by 5.5 percentage points and prevent the creation of 7.5 million jobs.

As banks realised their losses, they responded by restricting the availability of loans and credit to consumers, businesses and traders. This phenomenon, known as a credit crunch, meant that borrowers found it hard to get credit, which accelerated the fall in house prices and pushed many businesses to the wall. Governments across the developed world worked with the IMF to coordinate stimulus packages of $1 trillion of extra spending and injections of finance to offset the economic downturn. However the intervention left many countries nursing huge public deficits. In turn these became a concern and speculation over whether governments could avoid defaulting in turn led to the European debt crisis. The financial crisis that began in 2007 is still having its effect and some forecast a 'lost decade'. In July 2012 Sir Mervyn King, the Governor of the Bank of England, said he did not believe the UK was 'halfway through' the crisis.

International finance

The volatility in flows of money means that all countries suffer financial crises, just as many western countries did in 2007. As the Second World War was ending in 1944, the Allied powers decided an organisation was needed to oversee the international monetary system to ensure exchange rate stability and encourage members to eliminate exchange restrictions that hinder trade. During the Great Depression of the 1930s, countries had attempted to shore up their failing economies by raising barriers to foreign trade, devaluing their currencies to compete for export markets, and curtailing their citizens' freedom to hold foreign exchange. These attempts proved to be self-defeating.

> volatility in flows of money means that all countries suffer financial crises

Governments agreed to set up two sister organisations, the International Monetary Fund and the World Bank. The IMF is tasked in its own words 'to foster global monetary cooperation, secure financial stability, facilitate international trade, promote high employment and sustainable economic growth, and reduce poverty around the world'. The World Bank 'is a vital source of financial and technical assistance to developing countries around the world'. Both are intergovernmental bodies owned and run by their 188 country members.

The IMF has three main jobs. It carries out surveillance of the world economy and of the individual countries, producing four economic forecasts a year and detailed assessments of each of its members every two or three years. It provides technical assistance mainly to low- and middle-income countries on how to run and develop their economies, with advice on issues such as how to upgrade institutions, and how to design appropriate macroeconomic, financial and structural policies. Finally, it makes loans to countries that cannot meet their payments due to financial difficulties.

All these activities have led to bitter arguments about how it should operate and around the turn of the millennium large groups of protestors would turn up to its annual meetings in the spring and autumn to denounce its activities and particularly the advice it gives and the conditions it imposes on its loans. Critics also point out that it failed to predict the recent financial crisis.

The criticism centres on its advice and policies to countries hit by financial crisis. Its detractors, such as Nobel laureate economist Joseph Stiglitz, attacked what they called a 'Washington consensus' of privatisations, deregulation, cutting government spending through higher taxes and lower spending, and removing capital controls. They also condemned the institution as being non-transparent and not giving enough voice to poorer countries in the way it was run. They point to the way the IMF intervened in the Asian crisis of 1997 and the default of Argentina in 2001. More recently, leaders of emerging market countries in Asia, Africa and Latin America have highlighted the more lenient conditions attached to the bailouts of European countries hit by the 2010 crisis.

The IMF has said it learned lessons from its interventions in Asia and Latin America and from its work with African countries in order to improve the way it lends to countries in trouble and be better targeted and flexible. It says it has done a lot to improve the conditions it imposes on its lending programmes. It has also changed its thinking on putting up capital controls to protect against speculative capital (see box). It has also embarked on a process to give more votes on its decision-making body to emerging and developing economies.

 **example**

Return of capital controls

Since the onset of the 2007 financial crisis many emerging countries have put up capital controls to prevent volatile inflows and outflows of speculative investment. In 2010 the International Monetary Fund, which until then had advocated removing capital controls in order to attract investment, said there might be circumstances in which capital controls are a 'legitimate component of the policy response to surges in capital inflows'. One part of this new way of thinking was the experience of Malaysia after the whole of South East Asia was hit by a crisis in 1997. Initially Malaysia also voluntarily took on IMF-type policies of free movement of capital as well as rate hikes and spending cuts. As the situation worsened Malaysia rejected IMF advice and help and imposed capital controls and boosted spending. The IMF subsequently said that was the right decision.

The World Bank provides low-interest loans, interest-free credit and grants to developing countries, to support investments in such areas as education, health, public administration, infrastructure, financial and private sector development, agriculture, and environmental and natural resource management. It also provides policy advice, research and analysis, and technical assistance.

It has been criticised for funding major infrastructure projects such as dams and power stations that have brought nasty side effects such as pollution or the forced movement of local people as well as greater economic growth. It too has attracted protests by non-governmental organisations such as charities and think tanks in the past. The Bank was also criticised for working in partnership with the private sector and undermining the role of the state as the primary provider of essential goods and services, such as healthcare and education.

The Bank has made efforts to make its activities more transparent and, like the IMF, to reform the way that decisions are taken. It has also reformed its investment lending instrument in a way it says will strengthen effectiveness and developmental impact, improve compliance and increase accountability.

 **quotation**

The power of debt

In a detailed study of financial crises in 66 countries across five continents and over centuries two economists looked at the features shared by government defaults, banking panics, and inflationary spikes. The book, *This Time is Different*, which has won a number of awards, is named after a remark by an anonymous trader who said: 'More money has been lost because of four words than at the point of a gun – "this time is different".' Authors Carmen Reinhart and Kenneth Rogoff find that banking crises and bank failures often lead to defaults by sovereign governments on their debts.

Future of money

We will always need money but the rapid advance of technology has led people to ask whether notes and coins will soon become a thing of the past. Many people now do a lot of their banking online, paying their bills at the click of a few buttons rather than writing out a cheque or putting cash in an envelope. In fact there are plans in the UK to phase out cheques although those have been put on hold because of concerns of pensioners and of others with no access to the internet.

Technology has also enabled other financial innovations when it comes to using money. Not all of it is new. Paul Volcker, a former head of the US central bank, famously said that the most valuable financial innovation of the last 30 years was the ATM machine. More recent innovations include:

- **Smartcards for travel**. In London, commuters on the city's Tube, trains and buses can put money on an Oyster card that allows them to travel freely, debiting money as they pass through the ticket barriers. Many cities have similar schemes – a surprisingly large number with nautical names: Octopus (Hong Kong), Clipper (San Francisco), ORCA (Seattle), sQuid (Bolton, UK) and Walrus (Merseyside, UK).

- **Contactless payment using credit cards, debit cards, key fobs and even a watch**. The devices use radio frequency identification that allows people to pay by swiping their card – or watch – over a reader that picks up the signal and passes it on to the bank.

- **Mobile phones**. The first service that allows users to pay for purchases via their mobile phone has been launched in the UK. The Quick Tap payment system by phone operator Orange and Barclaycard credit cards allows users to make payments of up to £20. Others are sure to follow.

- **Local currencies**. Communities can set up currencies that can be exchanged for goods and services in the local area by people who agree to use them. In many ways it is akin to bartering as someone offering babysitting can earn credits that will allow them to buy goods. Examples include the TEM in the Greek port town of Velos, the BerkShare in Berkshire, Massachusetts, and the Bristol pound in the UK.

 example

Mobile phone banking

While western countries are usually seen as the drivers of financial innovations, there is one area where Africa has been leaps and bounds ahead of the rest of the world. Banking services have traditionally been sparse across the continent and ensuring that more citizens had bank accounts was part of a push to boost economic growth levels. For example, since 2007 M-Pesa in Kenya allows users to deposit and withdraw money from a nationwide network of agents operating out of small shops, petrol stations and other enterprises. M-Pesa has around 17 million registered users and handles around $21 million a day, mainly peer-to-peer transfers, but it is now being used to pay bills and other small transactions.

But there are signs that alternatives to traditional money could be on their way:

- **Bitcoin**. This digital currency is exchanged between users via computers. It does not have an issuing central bank or treasury and instead uses a computer network protocol to verify the transactions. The network is programmed to increase the money supply until the total number of bitcoins reaches an upper limit of about 21 million BTCs.

- **Gaming**. Computer-based games such as World of Warcraft, Second Life and Farmville use their own currencies that can be used as part of the game and, in the case of Second Life, can be converted back into US dollars.

- **Hub Culture**. A social network service that operates a global currency called the Ven. Users can buy, share and trade knowledge, goods and services globally with anyone in the network and these can be spent at any Hub Culture Pavilion. The value of the Ven is determined on the financial markets from a basket of currencies, commodities and carbon futures.

brilliant recap

- Money arose out of the need for a more efficient system of exchange than bartering.
- Money has three properties: a means of exchange, a store of value and a unit of account.
- Economists disagree over the exact nature of the link between the money supply and inflation.
- People need to borrow to make big purchases like cars and homes but recently household borrowing has risen sharply.
- Trillions of pounds, dollars and euros move through the financial system each day.
- Investors' search for high returns ultimately led to the sub-prime housing crash and the global financial crisis.
- Technology is enabling people to pay without using traditional money by using devices that send signals to the retailer and bank.
- Virtual currencies are run through private networks.

CHAPTER 9

Housing and property

'Buy land, they're not making it anymore'.

Mark Twain, American humourist, writer and lecturer, 1835–1910

A home is the most expensive asset anyone is likely to buy. House prices dominate dinner party debates, public policy and economic thinking in the UK. The buying, selling and borrowing against property has huge impacts on the economy and the property market has been linked to the last two downturns. Understanding how it works (and where it doesn't, such as with homelessness) is an essential part of seeing how economics works.

> the property market has been linked to the last two downturns

The housing market also has a major effect on the economy. An inadequate housing supply, or a poorly functioning housing market, constrains economic growth.

But not everyone owns their own home. Many people rent, either from a private landlord or from a public sector landlord. There is still a problem of homelessness even in countries that have high levels of GDP per head. And while homeownership is seen as a laudable ambition in countries such as the UK and US, it is less important in many countries on the European continent.

It is also important to point out that housing is only one form of property. Land can also be bought, sold and rented for use as farms, offices, factories, shops, government offices, airports and so on. These play a key role in the economy both in terms of their place in the property market and as important ingredients for economic growth. However, this chapter will focus on the housing market and primarily on how it operates in the UK.

An Englishman's home...

Housing is one of the most important issues where social needs can come into conflict with economics. A home is a fundamental human need. Economists call it a consumption good because everyone needs somewhere to live, but in a modern market economy it is also an asset that can be bought, sold, rented out and borrowed against. This means that in two separate ways it is subject to the basic laws of supply and demand and it has a price, whether it is the cost of buying the home or the price for renting it, and whether it is bought as a home or as an investment.

Before looking at how these markets operate it is worth looking at the different options available for living in a property – what the experts call 'housing tenure'. There are four broad groups:

- **Privately owned**: where the occupier owns the house outright or has bought it with the help of a loan from a bank (a mortgage).

- **Privately rented**: where the occupier does not own the home but instead pays a rent, usually weekly or monthly, to the landlord who owns the property.

- **Social housing**: where the occupant rents from a public sector organisation such as, in the UK, a local council or housing association.

- **Shared ownership**: where people who cannot afford the full purchase cost can buy a share and pay a rent to cover the remainder with an option to buy the rest at a later date. This is also known as partial purchase or part-buy, part-rent.

In the UK around 70% of homes are owner-occupied, which explains why house prices are such a hardy staple of dinner party conversations. But home ownership is very much a post-war phenomenon. In 1914 only one in 10 people owned their homes in the UK, with the vast majority renting properties and just a fraction in social housing. Owner-occupation rose on the back of speculative housing building and initiatives to promote mortgage finance to reach almost six out of 10 of people. The mass construction of council housing after the war saw social housing hit a peak of 30% in 1981. The 'right to buy' programme boosted home ownership as council tenants took advantage of incentives to buy their homes from their local councils.

The share of people who own their own homes varies across the major economies as Figure 9.1, illustrating national percentages taken from OECD figures for 2004, shows.

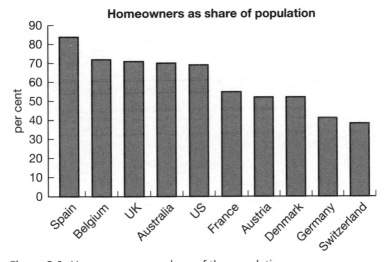

Figure 9.1 Homeowners as a share of the population
Source: Based on Dan Andrews and Aida Caldera Sanchez, 'Drivers of homeownership rates in selected OECD countries', Economics Department Working Papers No. 849, Organisation for Economic Co-operation and Development, 2011, Table 1, p. 9, www.oecd/org/eco/workingpapers

Despite the saying about an Englishman's home being his castle, the number of people owning their own home in the UK has fallen since the financial crisis. One estimate showed that the homeownership rate had fallen to 64.7% in 2012, its lowest rate since 1988. According to a report by Oxford Economics, the proportion of people living in owner-occupied homes in England will fall from a peak of 72.5% in 2001 to 63.8% in 2021.

 brilliant fact

The £300 million house

In September 2012 a 45-bedroom mansion overlooking London's Hyde Park was placed on the market at a record £300 million. The 60,000 square feet home was said to include a swimming pool, millions of pounds worth of gold leaf decoration and underground parking. The asking price was double the previous record for a property, also near Hyde Park, which sold in 2010 for £140 million. In the same year a parking space within walking distance of the famous stores Harrods and Harvey Nichols, and measuring just 12 by 23 feet, went on the market for £200,000.

What drives prices?

Like all other goods and services, the price of houses is driven by the laws of supply and demand. If more people want to buy the price will rise and if homebuilders respond by building new homes, the price should fall. However, houses are different from baked beans. There are a large number of other factors that affect both the supply and demand for homes, which sometimes makes it difficult to see what is going on.

> the price of houses is driven by the laws of supply and demand

The factors that will influence how keen and able people are to buy property include:

- **State of the economy**. Strong economic growth often leads to more jobs being created and higher wages being paid. The more people are earning, the more they will be able to commit to paying the mortgage bills. It will also lead to a greater willingness to make the 25-year commitment to a mortgage.

- **Interest rates**. As we saw in Chapter 7, the level of interest rates is key to determining mortgage rates. The mortgage rate will in turn determine how much money people feel that they can afford to borrow. A fall in interest rates, as happened in the wake of the recession of 2008–10, should encourage more people to buy property.

- **Access to credit**. Easier access to credit will make it easier for prospective buyers to get a mortgage. Banks will decide how much they are prepared to lend as a share of the value of the property and/or as a multiple of the buyer's or buyers' income. They may also raise or lower the fees involved.

- **Confidence**. If house prices rise in a consistent way, people are more likely to buy, both in the belief that they will carry on rising, and also out of fear that prices will eventually rise beyond their reach.

- **Speculation**. This is linked to the level of confidence – when investors decide that rising values and/or rents make housing look a better bet than alternative assets. In the long run this can contribute to a 'Minsky moment', as we saw in Chapter 8.

- **Taxes**. Governments sometimes use tax incentives to encourage people to buy a property. Many countries such as the UK do not impose a tax on any profit made when selling a home. Until 2000 the UK allowed borrowers tax relief on mortgage interest payments up to a certain limit.

Between 1983 and 1988 it allowed unmarried couples with joint mortgages to pool their allowances. Known as multiple mortgage tax relief, this was blamed for helping to fuel a rise in prices that ended with a price crash that began in 1989.

- **Social factors**. Changes in the population can also influence demand. Overall a rising population will increase demand for houses. This means that changes in birth rates and migration flows can influence prices. Changes in society such as higher divorce rates can support demand as it means more individuals will need to buy a home.

- **Rental market**. Renting property is an alternative to buying, and changes in rents can affect the demand for leasing over purchase. If property is cheap but rents are rising investors will buy homes in order to rent them out – known as buy-to-let.

Ultimately, the number of homes available will depend on the number of new properties being built and/or being available for sale or rent. There are many reasons why the supply of new homes does not react as quickly to changes in demand as they do in other sectors such as car and food production. These factors include:

- **Time lags**. There is often a gap between a change in price and an increase in the supply of new properties becoming available, or other homeowners deciding to put their properties onto the market. Economists say that changes in housing supply are 'inelastic' to price changes.

- **Planning constraints**. In most countries a builder cannot start work on a home until it has been given permission by a planning authority such as a local council. People living near a proposed site may object because they would prefer to have an open field near their home rather than a building site. These objections are often known by the acronym NIMBY (Not In My Back Yard). In the UK large areas of land that are protected from development are known as 'greenbelts'.

- **State of the economy**. Just as this will affect the number of people willing to buy, so it will impact on supply. Builders will be nervous about investing in building new homes if they are worried that they will struggle to find buyers at the right prices. Meanwhile existing owners will not put their homes up for sale if they fear they will get less for them than they believe they are worth.

- **Social housing**. Governments often build homes or subsidise charities to provide homes to ensure there is enough affordable housing. However, their ability to do this will depend on the state of the public finances and other political priorities. This will affect the total supply. For example, in the UK new social housing averaged over 130,000 a year in the 1950s and 1960s but then fell sharply, hitting a low of just 13,000 in 2003.

 **example**

Community land auctions

Academics have looked at ways of encouraging communities to embrace development. One proposal, by Tim Leunig at CentreForum, is for community land auctions. Local councils buy land from local landowners and then auction it – with planning permission – to developers. The increase in value is then returned to the local community. Another proposal, by Paul Cheshire of the LSE, is to give each adult a ration of 40 square metres with dependent children having another 20 square metres each, with a trading system to allow people to buy and sell. Finally, research from the LSE showing that planning constraints have kept house prices 35% higher than they would otherwise be have led to calls to relax controls on building on greenbelt land.

Rent or buy?

Much debate over housing focuses on owner-occupiers because of the impact that sector can have on the economy. Renting was once the dominant form of tenure for property in the UK and many other countries and high house prices are making it a more popular option.

Buying a home is attractive because the mortgage interest payments on most mortgages – other than those known as interest-only loans – go towards paying off the debt. Many people see this as better than renting, which is often described as pouring money down the drain. However, house buying is a long-term commitment and will suit people who want stability, are settled in a certain location and seek more control of decisions rather than people who are more likely to move in the short term, perhaps for a new job or training course. There is also the risk that the value of the property will fall even as the occupier has to carry on making the monthly mortgage payments.

Renting provides more flexibility as it only commits the person to the length of the lease. This is important if they know they are likely to move soon so can avoid the hassles of selling and buying a home – the time for searching, the legal costs and the risk of making a loss on the home sale. On the other hand, in some countries landlords have the power to raise the rent or ask their tenant to leave, which makes it harder for families to plan. Critics say this is a reason why the government needs to maintain an affordable social rented sector as a part of the mainstream housing system.

🔍 brilliant explanation

Explaining the fall in ownership

We saw earlier the decline in the share of Britons owning their own home. The factors behind demand and supply go a long way to explaining that. Homes have become less affordable especially for first-time buyers because increases in house prices have outstripped rises in wages over the last few decades. The financial crisis has made banks and building societies become more cautious about the terms on which they offer mortgages. High levels of debt mean people are less willing to take out a mortgage. There is a shortage of new homes coming onto the market to match the increase in population. For example, house building in the UK fell by 4% in the year to August 2012.

Measuring prices

Given the importance of house prices, both to homeowners' personal financial health and to the efforts of politicians and central bankers to keep the economy on an even keel, it is important to have accurate figures. Many developing economies have a range of measures and certainly in the UK the number of house price indices have been rising almost as rapidly as property values!

The two main indices in the UK are published by Halifax and Nationwide, two of the largest mortgage lenders in the country. Each uses its own transactions data, which are large enough to be a representative indicator of what is going on in the country. The aim is to produce one standardised index of house prices. The problem is that no two houses are identical and may differ according to a variety of characteristics relating to the physical attributes of the houses themselves or to their locations. By breaking down the figures according to a range of characteristics such as the type of property and the region, and according to different figures such as the number of bedrooms, bathrooms and garages and the age of the property, the analysts can track how the prices of the same types of homes have changed.

One problem is that there is a time lag between the decision to buy the property and when the transaction gets logged. Figures from Halifax and Nationwide are based on mortgage transactions at the time they are approved rather than when they are completed. Indices produced by the government are based on completed transactions, which can be several weeks or months after the property went on sale. One innovation has been to track the price of properties that come onto the market to see what sellers are asking for their homes. Since this tracks prices right at the beginning of the selling process it can give an indication of the future direction of the housing market.

brilliant history

The Monopoly board game

Millions of families have sat down to a game of Monopoly, the board game made up of famous streets in cities from New York to Gdynia in Poland. All the players start equal but, through luck and skill, the winner will end up owning all the property on the board. Few will know that the game was designed in the late 1800s by Elizabeth Magie, an American woman who was inspired by the writings of her father Henry George. George had blamed the monopoly ownership of land for high levels of poverty. The game was therefore a way of showing how that could occur without intervention or regulation.

Housing and the economy

Economists study house prices because they can have a huge influence on other trends such as consumer spending and borrowing. When house prices rise, this can lead to a rise in confidence among consumers who feel they become wealthier. This can encourage them to spend more, which can lead to faster economic growth and inflation. This process can become circular as the improved

house prices can have a huge influence on other trends

economic conditions make people more willing to take out a loan to buy a property. This effect can be compounded by something known as 'mortgage equity withdrawal' (MEW), where homeowners can borrow money against the increased value of their home.

brilliant explanation

Mortgage equity withdrawal

The rapid rise in house prices between the early 1990s and 2008 meant that many homeowners became much wealthier. However this gain was only on paper and would not normally be turned into cash until they sold their property. The phenomenon became so significant on both sides of the Atlantic that it came to be known as using one's home as an ATM (automatic teller machine). By taking out a new mortgage against their property they could get their hands on the cash. As well as funding spending MEW was used to pay off debt, add to homeowners' pension pots or was due to older people moving to a smaller property after their children had left home.

When house prices fall this process can go into reverse as consumers cut spending to offset the fall in wealth. This can feed through to job cuts and business closures and a wider economic slowdown that will exacerbate the fall in house prices. If people are unable to meet the mortgage payments they will be in danger of losing their homes – known as repossession. If the fall in prices takes the value of the home below the size of the mortgage loan against it then they are said to be in negative equity. This means they are unable to sell their home and move without crystallising the loss.

Between the autumn of 2007 and the spring of 2009, house prices fell in pure cash terms by around 20% in the UK. The Bank of England has estimated that around 7–11% of owner-occupier mortgage holders were in negative equity in the spring of 2009, although for most of those households, the total value of negative equity was relatively small.

The link between house prices, consumer spending and economic growth is hotly debated. Some economists believe that there are common factors driving both house prices and spending and the changes in both – whether up or down – happening at the same time does not show a link between the two. Examples of these factors include changes in interest rates, changes in the ease of access to mortgage credit and changes in people's confidence driven by outside events. But it is clear that rises in house prices are associated with better economic times and vice versa.

> rises in house prices are associated with better economic times and vice versa

Bubble trouble

Assets such as houses are prone to price bubbles. While there is no single definition, they tend to occur when rises in house prices due to fundamental economic reasons, such as greater confidence, higher incomes and lower borrowing costs, are followed by a wave of speculative buying. This is often based on a belief that past patterns are a guide to the future and that prices will carry on rising. Given the important role of housing as a home, this encourages aspiring homeowners to worry they will miss out if they do not buy soon. Behavioural economists have also noticed a tendency for people to join in a rush to buy, which they call the 'herd' instinct.

Economists worry about bubbles because they lead to a huge accumulation of debt on the way up and a large amount of misery on the way down that extends beyond the victims themselves. For this reason there has long been a debate about whether policymakers should 'prick' a bubble. The argument in favour of raising interest rates to slow a booming housing market will cause pain for some homebuyers and it will prevent the more ruinous impact from a crash. Critics say that it is better to use regulation to impose tighter lending standards and lower limits on the amount people can borrow as a share of their income or the asking price of the house.

In the wake of the financial crisis and crash in house prices, regulators in the US and Europe are proposing much tighter regulations. These could involve setting limits on the size of the loan to the value of the property (loan-to-value ratio or LTI) or on the ratio of the buyer's income to the home value (loan-to-income or LTI). An alternative is to make banks that offer high LTV or LTI loans hold more capital to give them a greater cushion if house prices fall. Advocates say this will make the system safer while critics say it will make it harder for people to buy homes and may mean lower economic growth. One rule of thumb is that increasing the amount of capital that banks need to keep in reserve by 1 percentage point relative to their loans will push up interest rates by as much as 15 basis points -- 0.15 percentage points. On the other hand it is likely to lead to a fall in the number of 'bad' loans.

Why housing matters

There are other reasons why having a well-functioning housing market is important to economists. Good housing affects our quality of life, our health and our wellbeing. Research has shown that its impact on people's health and happiness lead to higher achievement by children in school and can even lead to lower rates of crime.

However, a failure to ensure there are enough homes will have negative consequences. Shortages of homes at prices that workers can afford to buy or rent will affect the ability of people to move home to take up new jobs. At the more extreme end of the problem homelessness creates wider costs to the public purse in the form of weak job prospects, higher social security benefits, poor health and crime.

Housing also affects the health of the national economy. It can enhance economic performance and place competitiveness. However, in areas of high demand, the high costs of living will impose costs of doing business by raising wages and rent levels, and impacting on business location and expansion decisions. Businesses can be affected by problems of housing affordability. High house prices will prevent people from moving home in order to find and take jobs. Alternatively workers have to travel very long commuter distances to get to and from work, which adds to congestion and hits their quality of life. That can have long-term implications for economic growth and sustainability.

A flexible housing system that offers adequate supplies of a range of housing, including high quality rental stock and social housing as well as owner-occupied properties, is an ingredient for sustaining growth and labour market mobility, ensuring that overcrowding does not cause social problems, providing housing opportunities for households to move through their individual life cycles.

Housebuilding can contribute to economic growth and job creation. Professor Stephen Nickell, an economist who once served on the Bank of England's interest rate setting committee, has said building 100,000 new homes over four years may add 0.3 percentage points to economic growth. Assuming that each new property is valued at £200,000, these extra 25,000 homes a year will be worth an additional £5 billion a year.

 brilliant recap

- Housing is a basic human need but it is also an economic asset.
- It includes privately owned homes, rented homes and social housing.
- A range of factors affect demand for housing.
- The supply of new homes can take a long time to respond to increases in demand.
- Housing is vulnerable to swings between booms and busts.
- A well-functioning housing market is good for economic growth.

CHAPTER 10

Trade and currencies

'The propensity to truck, barter and exchange one thing for another is common to all men, and to be found in no other race of animals'.

Adam Smith, philosopher and economist, 1723–90

f you are reading this on a mobile device or an e-reader, please turn over the device and see where it was made. I will bet a pound to a penny it will say 'Made in China'. Check the label on your t-shirt and there is a fair chance it was woven in Bangladesh. Most western families can probably find several hundred items made in China or elsewhere in the world in their home.

Trade is as old as civilisation itself. Cave paintings and archaeological remains indicate that humans have been trading with each other for thousands of years. Nor is international trade a new concept. The Silk Road provided a conduit for trade between China and the West many centuries before that country's factories started producing most of the developed world's electronic goods and toys and even paperclips.

But while we take the benefits of these trades for granted, few people understand the complex economic relationships that influence which goods and services countries trade with each other, the prices at which they buy and sell and how this influences – and is influenced by – exchange rates. But among those who have taken the time to study the subject there are some who have become very angry at the inequalities they say that the international trade system brings to certain groups of people and parts of the world.

Trading places

At its most basic level, trade allows people to get their hands on goods that they could not otherwise have. As we saw in Chapter 8 people have bartered from the earliest times, so that someone who could make horseshoes could exchange their output for grain from a farmer. Bartering led to the creation of money, which made it easier for people to trade with each other by using money to buy and sell what they wanted. And just as this model fits for the medieval blacksmith and farmer so it applies to modern households, corporations and countries.

> trade allows people to get their hands on goods that they could not otherwise have

International trade today differs from those barter exchanges carried out centuries ago in terms of the speed, volume, geographic reach, complexity and diversity of the transactions. But the fundamental idea of trading goods and services in exchange for money still applies.

Why countries trade

If there were no such thing as trade, life would be pretty monotonous and limited. People in a country like Britain would live on a diet of root vegetables, bread and meat, drink mead (a drink made from honey) and wear clothes made from hemp and other locally grown materials. In other words, life would be fairly similar to that in pre-Roman Britain. Contrast that with today's lifestyles and it is clear that we benefit from trade. This helps explain why companies are happy to deal with the logistical and legal complications that come with trade.

Trade is made up of exports – goods and services we sell to others – and imports – those that we buy from firms in other countries. Countries export because they find that they are able to produce more of a particular item than is needed at home and so can sell the excess overseas. These sales in turn raise money that will allow spending on goods and services that they would prefer. They may also be able to sell their goods at a higher price than they can get in their domestic market.

The goods and services that a country can export will depend on the same factors that drive economic growth: natural resources, physical capital, human resources and technology. For example, large natural resource supplies, such as the crude oil reserves underneath many of the Middle Eastern states, will make those countries energy exporters. Countries with large areas of land and a climate suited to growing crops will export food, as happens in Africa and Asia. Developed countries with the factories and technology that enable them to invent and manufacture more sophisticated products and services will focus on those.

Countries also like to import for the reverse of the reasons that they export. They will need to buy goods and services that their citizens either need for basic existence, or they want but which cannot be made locally. They will also want to import those goods and services that are cheaper or better than those produced domestically. In the UK, wine would fall into the former category (with respect to English wine growers) while a whole range of manmade goods and services will fall into the latter.

Comparative advantage

With the exception of natural resources, many countries could probably produce most of the goods that consumers want but the quality and price of those goods would make some of them very unattractive. The way that economists look at this is through the concept of 'comparative advantage'. This was set out by David Ricardo, the 18th century English economist, whom we met in Chapter 1.

He was inspired by reading the theory of the division of labour that Adam Smith set out in the *Wealth of Nations* and sought to apply it to international trade. He was thinking and writing at the time of the Corn Laws, which parliament passed to impose large tariffs on cheaper imported grain in order to protect English landowners. The resulting higher prices caused riots in towns across England and anger among manufacturers who were forced to raise workers' wages.

Comparative advantage is one of the most important concepts in economics and probably the idea that is best known by non-economists. But it is also hard for people to get their head round because it is initially counter-intuitive. Ricardo posed the issue in the context of two countries, Portugal and England, that produce both cloth and wine. But to bring it more up to date let's look at a fictitious example for two South East Asian countries that both make DVD players and televisions.

---

brilliant example

South Korea can produce 1,000 mp3 players an hour and 1,000 headphones. Thailand has broken into the market and can now make 200 mp3 players and 500 headphones. So between them in an hour they turn out 1,200 mp3 players and 1,500 headphones or 2,700 in total. Quite simply, South Korea is better at making both (an absolute advantage in economics) and many non-economists would think they should carry on making both and exporting them to Thailand. However, Thailand only has to sacrifice making 200 mp3 players to make another 500 headphones – the opportunity cost we learned in Chapter 1 – but would lose making 500 headphones to make another 200 mp3s. It has a comparative advantage in switching to headphones – at 1,000 an hour. To fill the market South Korea can convert the headphone factory into making mp3s, making 2,000 an hour. Total production now rises from 2,700 an hour to 3,000. Total output has risen. Because the Thais are more productive at making headphones they will earn more in wages than they did in the mp3 factory so income will also rise, further fuelling growth.

Subsequently two economists, Eli Heckscher and Bertil Ohlin, decided to extend the theory by looking at countries' comparative advantage in terms of the factors of production such as labour, skills, machinery and so on. A country with large resources of low-skilled labour can produce goods that countries with a better skilled, and so higher paid, workforce would produce at a much higher cost. In return, that country can export back to the low-skilled economy the high quality goods and service that it can produce more efficiently. This helps explain why insurers based in the UK might wish to outsource back-office call centres to India (effectively importing the low-skilled labour) while successfully exporting insurance contracts.

New trade theory

The final stop on our journey through trade models is the 'new trade theory' (NTT), which despite its name was put forward by Nobel laureate economist Paul Krugman in the 1960s and 1970s and later updated by him in the early 1990s. NTT highlights the fact that larger

> larger companies are better able to exploit economies of scale

companies are better able to exploit economies of scale and produce goods at a lower cost than many small firms.

This implies that early entrants into a market can quickly build a comparative advantage over other countries which would then be well advised to look at other industries. While this is likely to result in a series of oligopolies – markets dominated by just a few players – or monopolies, this will still be good for consumers as prices will still be lower than if a greater number of products were produced by a myriad of less efficient companies. NTT advocates argue that this justifies government intervention to use selective subsidies on domestic start-ups and protective tariffs against competitors to allow the industry to flourish.

 **brilliant** explanation

The NTT explains both why Japan has a strong car industry and also why Germany and Japan trade cars with each other. The Japanese car industry would almost certainly not have become as successful as it was without some level of protection by its government after the Second World War. Because car production requires a lot of investment you will end up with a small number of large competitors that still offer enough variety and competition for Germans to choose to buy Japanese cars and vice versa. The same model explains why the world has two dominant makers of wide-bodied aeroplanes – Boeing and Airbus – which compete aggressively against each other.

Deficit and surplus

Countries that trade with each other will send a lot of money overseas buying goods and services they do not make (or at least not cheaply enough) and will receive inflows of money from overseas buyers. The difference between a country's imports and exports tells you whether it has a trade deficit or surplus. This figure often appears on the news in the UK and US as those two countries have both run up considerable deficits in recent years.

In order to get a clearer idea of what is going on, statisticians divide the overall balance into the trade in goods and services. For instance, the UK has a surplus in services due to its strength in areas such as financial services, insurance and entertainment but a deficit in goods. Since the goods deficit outstrips the surplus the UK has a net trade deficit. As we saw in Chapter 2, this then feeds through to the GDP figures, effectively subtracting (or adding in the case of a surplus) from the final estimate for economic growth.

A country will also receive money from the operations and investments of its companies overseas while earnings on investments by foreign companies in the UK will flow back. The net investment income is then added to the trade balance along with transfer payments (such as those that go between the UK and EU) to produce the current account balance.

The final piece of the jigsaw is the capital account, which is made up of the balance between money going overseas in the form of overseas takeovers or purchases of foreign investments such as bonds and capital coming in. The current account and capital account must technically balance to zero. For example, a country running a current account deficit will need to borrow money to fund that shortfall.

As a deficit in one country must be matched with surpluses somewhere else, very high deficits can lead to tensions between countries on the other side of that equation. In the US there has been growing concern about its trade deficit with China, which exports a vast range of goods to the US. In 2012 the US racked up a $315 billion trade deficit. China uses a large amount of the dollar revenues it receives to buy US government bonds known as treasuries. As of November 2012 China was holding $1.17 trillion in treasuries. This has led to fears that if China ever decided to sell down its holding this would cause a collapse in the price which – as we saw in Chapter 6 – would send the yield of interest rates soaring and plunge the US into recession. Most economists believe China would avoid such a mutually assured destruction.

 **brilliant** example

In 2005, when the booming US economy was sucking in exports from China, public concern over the deficit was starting to rise. On 1 January one American family pledged to live a year without having anything in the house that was made in China. Journalist Sara Bongiorni recorded the experience in a book, *A Year Without Made in China*, which follows the family's discovery of the sheer quantity of Chinese-made goods they owned. Once they made the decision to go cold turkey on China they realised how resourceful they had to be to source items they needed by making substitutions and being more inventive. As Georgetown University economist Pietra Rivoli, author of the book about a t-shirt's global journey whom we shall meet later, said in her review: 'The myriad moral complexities in the relationship between American consumers and Chinese factory are evident in each shopping trip.'

Currencies and exchange rates

Anyone who has travelled abroad knows they will need to take money in the form of notes and coins that can be used in the other country. People who take overseas holidays are, in an economist's view, importing a leisure service. The same applies to companies trading overseas. In order to sell their goods and services overseas they will be paid in that country's currency. Similarly, importers will need to pay their supplier in a different currency.

This means that companies on both sides of the trade need to know how much their currency is worth in terms of their partner's currency. For example a UK company making boats may need to import an engine from Germany. The German firm says that the engine costs €100,000. If the exchange rate is 80p to the euro then the UK firm will need to send €80,000 to

Germany. When the boat is built the UK firm finds an American buyer for its £1 million craft. Since the exchange rate is $1.50 to the pound, the buyer needs to find $1.5 million to secure the purchase.

The relationship between one currency and another is known as the exchange rate. The problem for traders is that these exchange rates move on a daily basis. The value of one currency against another will vary according to currency traders' views about the prospects for both economies. One of the major factors that influence the exchange rate is the official interest set by the central bank, as we saw in Chapter 7. If one country raises its interest rates then people investing in that currency will get a greater return. Exchange rates will rise even if traders *suspect* that a central bank will raise interest rates at a time when other countries are not.

Another factor is inflation. When currency traders believe that a nation is heading for a bout of inflation in the near future, they are likely to sell their holdings of that currency. This is because inflation, as we saw in Chapter 6, reduces the value of the money in terms of what it can buy, therefore making it less valuable compared to its non-inflationary neighbour's currency. The trade balance will also affect the exchange rate. A country with a trade deficit has to buy more of other countries' currencies than overseas traders are buying of theirs. Finally, countries suffering political instability will see their exchange rates fall as traders and investors feel less confident about doing business there.

> exchange rates will affect exporters and importers in opposite ways

Movements in exchange rates will affect exporters and importers in opposite ways. Taking the UK as an example, a rise in the value of sterling against currencies of other countries –

which economists call appreciation – will make its exports more expensive to overseas buyers because those firms will need to use more of their currency to buy the pounds needed to buy the goods. However, it will make imports cheaper because UK firms will need fewer pounds to pay foreign currency needed to pay the supplier. Depreciation works the other way round – better for exports but worse for imports.

brilliant fact

In the run-up to Christmas 2007 the pound was worth $2.11, having bought just $1.50 a couple of years earlier. This prompted news stories about people flying to New York for festive shopping trips in the knowledge that the savings on their Christmas presents paid for the cost of their trip to the US. After the onset of the financial crisis the pound fell more than 30% against the euro between February and December 2008, making it cheaper for Europeans to come to the UK.

Companies can protect themselves from movements in currencies by using a technique known as 'hedging'. While the technique is quite complicated, the principle is simple: taking a financial bet that will pay out if the exchange rate moves against you. Hedging is done by buying a derivative, which is an option to buy or sell a currency at a certain level in the future. An exporter might be worried that sterling will rise against the euro and that he will receive less from sales. By buying the right to buy sterling and sell euros in the future at today's prices, if sterling does rise he will make a profit on that bet. That profit will offset the loss on his sales as a result of the rise in sterling.

Half-pound burgers

The example above highlights a problem with understanding what exchange rates mean. The shopping trip to New York was a bargain because while the exchange rate had moved, the prices of the actual goods had not. In other words the exchange rate in the *bureau de change* does not represent what is happening on the ground. If the identical top-of-the-range computer costs $1,500 in New York and £1,000 in London then the exchange rate should be $1.5 to the pound (or 67p to the dollar). If the exchange rate is actually $2 to the pound (50p to the dollar) then the British tourist only needs £750 to buy it.

Economists say this shows that the pound is overvalued and the dollar is undervalued. In order to gauge what the 'real' exchange rate is economists use a concept known as purchasing power parity (PPP). This is measured by taking the same basket of goods and services and seeing how much they cost in all the different countries of the world. The theory of PPP says that exchange rates should eventually adjust to make the price of a basket of goods the same in each country.

This avoids the impact of the economic forces that can make *bureau de change* exchange rates fluctuate. PPP makes it easier to compare GDP between different countries as a sharp fall in the exchange rate will make it appear that a country's economy has contracted when in fact in PPP terms it may have risen. The International Monetary Fund produces estimates of the GDP of its member countries in US dollars in both the nominal and PPP exchange rates. This means that if, for example, the Thai bhat halves in value against the dollar, the PPP index will show that the size of the economy has not halved, as it would appear using the floating exchange rate.

However, PPP has its own problems. It is difficult to take into account different purchasing patterns – for example, that people in poor countries will spend more of their income on food than those in wealthier countries who will spend more on housing and entertainment. Similar products may be of very different quality between two countries. Furthermore, in some cases, such as food, one has to compare wholly different products. While rice is a staple food in Asia it is not found in parts of Africa, where cassava is a primary food source.

 **brilliant** example

Big Mac index

In 1986 *The Economist* magazine came up with a basket of goods and services to compare currencies with just one item – the Big Mac. It measures the price of a Big Mac hamburger sold at McDonald's restaurants around the world, and then compares those prices to the exchange rate of those currencies. For example in July 2012 a Big Mac, which sold for $4.33 in America, cost just $2.29 (75 roubles) in Russia, whereas in Brazil it sold for just under $5 (10 reals).

Protect and survive?

Given the importance of exports to an economy and inflows of capital it is perhaps no surprise that governments will use policies to support those industries. But how far should governments go? One of the lessons from the Great Depression of the 1930s was that attempts by governments to protect their industries not only failed to work but made the crisis even worse.

The idea of trying to protect a country's export industry and employment or prevent imports from coming in goes by the peculiar name of 'beggar-thy-neighbour' policies. It is also known as protectionism. This tends to involve two tactics: restricting imports by raising barriers and imposing tariffs; or artificially devaluing the currency to make exports cheaper for overseas buyers and imports more expensive for domestic firms. The aim is to boost one's economy at the expense of others.

The danger is that while one country might get a head start by moving first, other countries will soon retaliate. The British Keynesian economist Joan Robinson pointed out after the Depression that while an artificially induced increase in exports relative to imports will create more jobs and boost the spending power of those workers, it will have the opposite effect on other countries' economies. As everyone pulls up the barriers the volume of world trade falls and the world economy contracts.

That lesson seemed to have been learned during the crisis that began in 2007/08. As the scale of the downturn became apparent, leaders of the largest economies agreed at a summit of the Group of 20 (G20) in London in April 2009 to work together to stimulate the economy and to refrain from protectionism. However, more recently there have been signs of tensions. As we saw in Chapter 7, countries such as the UK, the US and Japan have sought to boost their economies by injecting money into the system (the policy known as quantitative easing). This has tended to cause their currencies to fall and led countries whose exchange rates have risen to accuse them of protectionism. In September 2010, the finance minister of Brazil, Guido Mantega, coined the phrase 'international currency wars' to describe those policies.

> while one country might get a head start by moving first, other countries will soon retaliate

Free trade...

The experiences of the 1930s also led politicians to work together to set up a formal system that would help to reduce tariff barriers by making it harder for governments to stop imports either by putting up taxes or setting tough conditions on importers. This led to the General Agreement on Tariffs and Trade (GATT), a multilateral agreement signed by 23 countries in 1947. A series of negotiations between the growing number of members organised on a one-country-one-vote basis – often given the name multilateralism – led to a pronounced reduction in the number of tariff barriers and a decline in taxes on imports, particularly industrial goods. This process culminated in the creation of the World Trade Organisation in 1995, which was also given the power to arbitrate in the case of trade disputes.

However this focus on reducing industrial tariffs led to growing anger among non-governmental groups such as anti-poverty charities and academics who said there was not enough focus on the barriers faced by developing countries in their exports of agricultural products and textiles, which are the mainstays of many of those economies. In his book *Globalization and its Discontents*, Nobel laureate economist Joseph Stiglitz, a former chief economist at the World Bank, accused the WTO of preaching fair trade while imposing crippling economic policies on developing nations. It also fuelled a popular campaign against the WTO and globalisation, which were seen as making conditions worse for poorer people. This culminated in the so-called 'battle of Seattle' of September 1999 when the third conference of the WTO ended in failure amid scenes of skirmishes between protestors and police on the streets of the American city.

Two years later, at a summit in the Qatari capital Doha in November 2001, ministers signed up to a whole new round of negotiations. This was called the Doha Development Round and was explicitly aimed at making globalisation more inclusive and at helping the world's poor, particularly by slashing barriers and subsidies in agriculture. However, more than 10 years and several failed summits later, there is little sign of an overarching new trade deal that would deliver welfare gains ranging from $84 billion to $574 billion according to various estimates.

 **brilliant** explanation

Globalisation is the name given to the system that allows people and companies across the world to trade with others and invest in each other's countries. The word made it into *Webster's Dictionary* in 1961. However, in recent years it also has become a term of abuse. Critics such as Stiglitz say that while it has created wealth it has increased inequality and much of the benefits have accrued to largely western multinational corporations. Advocates such as the writer Thomas Friedman, author of the book *The World is Flat*, say that freer trade has helped make millions of people wealthier. They say globalisation can take some credit for China hitting the United Nations' target of halving the number of poor people from the 1990 figure of 85 million.

...and fair trade

The criticism of globalisation and its side effects have led some consumers in the West to pay more attention to how the items they buy in their local shops are made. This trend is particularly focused on ensuring that producers of foods and clothing receive the full financial benefit of their work and do not suffer as a result of trading with multinational organisations, with, for example, damage to their local environment.

There is no official definition of 'fair trade' and a number of organisations have been set up to provide advice to consumers and in some cases give labels to goods that they say meet their standards, particularly that the producers receive a decent wage. Bodies that issue certificates include Traidcraft and Fairtrade. Two goods that have attracted a particular focus on fair trade are bananas from the Caribbean and Latin America, and coffee from Africa and South America. According to estimates made in 2005, global fair trade sales had reached €1.1 billion, increasing at rates of around 50% per year. Fair trade bananas had a market share of 56% in Switzerland while the US fair trade coffee market has been growing nearly 90% per year since fair trade coffee was launched in 1998.

brilliant example

In 1999 Dr Rivoli, the economist who reviewed the *A Year Without Made in China* book, was inspired to track the origins of a t-shirt after hearing a protestor talking about appalling working conditions at an Indian clothes factory. She followed the origins of a $6 t-shirt she found on offer in a branch of Walgreen's in Fort Lauderdale, Florida. It turned out the cotton was harvested near Lubbock, Texas, and sent to textile mills in Shanghai, China, where it was spun, woven and sewn before being transported back to Miami. There it was imprinted with logos and graphics by the importer and then delivered to Walgreen's. After wearing it out Dr Rivoli took it to a Salvation Army bin in Maryland. It was then bought by a small entrepreneur and sold into the used clothing market in Tanzania.

More recently consumers have become concerned about the environmental damage done by importing goods from hundreds or even thousands of miles away. Food miles (or kilometres) describe the distance that food is transported as it travels from producer to consumer. For exotic tropical fruit this can be several thousands of miles. Concern over the impact on the environment from the carbon emission created by the long flights or boat journeys to import the fruit has led some consumers to choose locally produced goods.

Fair trade is not a recent fad. A blue Wedgwood sugar bowl dating from 1825 in the British Museum has an emotive measure etched onto it as a decoration: 'East India sugar not made by slaves. By six families using East India instead of West India sugar, one less slave is required.' This is a good example of the marketing – as well as ethical – power fair trade can have. Consumers frequently use their spending power to force organisations to abandon suppliers accused of poor standards by organising a boycott.

However, the fair trade movement has attracted criticism from both sides of the political debate. On the right, advocates of free trade say that fair trade makes up a tiny share of global trade and distracts from the need to liberalise trade so that countries can move up the value chain from agriculture towards more lucrative activities. They also accuse them of applying western standards to developing countries that could not afford to meet those standards. For example – and this is controversial – prohibition on child labour may not always be best for poor families.

On the left, critics say that it trivialises an important issue by making it an act of philanthropy for consumers to choose one product over another. They are concerned that consumers are not in a position to analyse whether a particular product is genuinely fair trade, creating a risk that consumers may be hoodwinked by traders who actually keep most of the higher price that fair trade products attract. They also believe that resolving inequities in global trade involves action by politicians to stop businesses taking advantage of indigenous peoples.

 **brilliant** recap

- People have traded since time immemorial to obtain goods and services they could not otherwise have.

- Countries will also trade in goods with another country that can make things cheaper and better.

- The doctrine of comparative advantage explains why countries should always specialise in the things they can do best.

- Countries that import more than they export have a trade deficit. This has to be paid for by borrowing from overseas.

- Exchange rates make exports more expensive and imports cheaper.

- The Great Depression taught politicians that putting trade barriers up during a downturn makes economic conditions worse rather than better.

- Since 1944 countries have made agreements to bring down barriers to trade.

- Western consumers have become more concerned that the people who make or harvest the goods they buy get a fair deal.

CHAPTER 11

The future of economics

'Classic economic theory, based as it is on an inadequate theory of human motivation, could be revolutionised by accepting the reality of higher human needs.'

Abraham Maslow, American psychologist, 1908–70

Economics has had a bad press in the wake of the financial crisis, and perhaps rightly so. But the criticism of the failure of all but a handful of economists to foresee the greatest economic disaster for generations feeds into a wider critique of economics with its focus on the 'rational agents' and the logic that led to Sir Thomas Carlyle branding it the 'dismal science' in response to the grim predictions by Malthus that we saw in Chapter 1. While there are many separate attacks made on mainstream economics it was perhaps best summarised more recently in the words of Gordon Gekko, the anti-hero of the 1987 film *Wall Street*, who declared: 'Greed is good. Greed is right. Greed works.'

The idea that people act in their self-interest and respond purely to price signals does not sound very attractive even if it does help us to understand how markets operate. However, it struggles to explain charitable donations, tipping in restaurants, evidence that money does not buy happiness or when people behave in ways that economics would deem irrational. Furthermore, the reduction of human interactions to a series of complex equations involving algebraic notations that only cognoscenti understand has alienated many people from economics. To paraphrase Oscar Wilde's definition of a cynic in the *Portrait of Dorian Gray*, many people see economists as people who know the price of everything and the value of nothing.

Part of the problem is with the way that economics is measured. While gross domestic product may or may not be an accurate measure of economic output, it does not capture elements of an economy that make us worse off, such as pollution, or any measure of whether people in that economy are more or less happy than they were earlier. The good news is that there has been a lot of radical thinking inside the economics profession for many years, motivated by a desire to ensure that economics can explain and understand human behaviour and help devise solutions to the world's most serious problems.

All in the mind

One of the most significant developments in economics in recent decades has been the crossover between that discipline and psychology. Economists have realised that we are not all perfectly rational agents all the time, responding to incentives and pursuing goals consistently without mistakes. Research has shown that people exhibit the same irrational responses and make the – rationally speaking – wrong choices in given circumstances again and again.

This appears to contradict the idea of the 'rational agents' which we met in Chapter 1 and which is key to the original thinking behind first microeconomics and then macroeconomics. If people do not always behave exactly as a

we are not all
perfectly rational
agents all the time

model based on financial incentives would predict, then understanding the psychology behind these other motives and triggers needs to become part of our thinking about how the economy works. Critics of the assumption of rationality such as Dan Ariely point to the 2008/09 global financial crisis as something that was the result of the fact that 'psychology and irrational behaviour play a much larger role in the economy's functioning than rational economists have been willing to admit'.

Thinkers who have combined economics and psychology are known as behavioural economists. Although it's a relatively new discipline within economics one of its key disciples, Daniel Kahneman, has won the Nobel prize for economics, while books by three of its other proponents – Steven Levitt, Richard Thaler and Ariely – have become famous across the world through their best-selling books (*Freakonomics*, *Nudge* and *Predictably Irrational*, respectively).

There are three key concepts at the heart of behavioural economics that have complicated names but which help show what often prevents people from making rational decisions, despite their best efforts. The first is known as 'bounded rationality'. This says that humans do try to make rational rather than arbitrary decisions when it comes to money – and other aspects of life – but that this rationality is limited, or bounded, by a tendency towards mental short cuts.

These short cuts are known as 'heuristics', which are intuitive equations of thought processes that we develop over time to reach a rough answer to a particular question. Quite often heuristics, which comes from the ancient Greek word meaning to find, are helpful as they enable us to make sense of a complex environment relatively quickly. However, there are many times when they prevent us from making a correct assessment of the world and lead us into making the wrong decision.

When that happens, it can lead to 'cognitive biases', a concept set out in 1972 by Kahneman and his fellow academic Amos Tversky, both psychologists rather than economists. This is the tendency to use and process information by filtering it through one's own likes, dislikes and experiences and drawing incorrect conclusions that might seem irrational. When it comes to financial decisions these mistakes can be costly for both the individual and the economy.

 **quotation**

Dan Ariely says that behavioural economics came of age on 23 October 2008. Giving evidence to the US Congress the former Federal Reserve chairman Alan Greenspan said he had 'found a flaw' in free-market economic theory. He said: 'I made a mistake in presuming that the self-interests of organisations, specifically banks and others, were such that they were best capable of protecting their own shareholders and their equity in the firms when a massive earthquake reduced the financial world to rubble.' Writing in the *Harvard Business Review* six months later Ariely said: 'We are now paying a terrible price for our unblinking faith in the power of the invisible hand. We're painfully blinking awake to the falsity of standard economic theory – that human beings are capable of always making rational decisions and that markets and institutions, in the aggregate, are healthily self-regulating.'

Heuristics you need to know

Decades of research and experiments by psychologists and economists have led to the identification of a large number of individual biases. Wikipedia, the online encyclopaedia, listed a total of 169 as of February 2013 and it is such a lively area of research that more will doubtless have been added by the time you read this. It is not possible to list all of them but it is useful to highlight some key principles that link them together and pick highlights of the heuristics that people most commonly fall victim to and which can be exploited by economic policymakers for positive benefits.

The New Economics Foundation, an independent think tank that aims to focus on real economic well-being, identified a number of core principles of behavioural economics:

- **Other people's behaviour matters**. People do many things by observing others and copying, and are encouraged to continue to do things when they feel other people approve of their behaviour.

- **People are creatures of habit**. People do many things without consciously thinking about them. Old habits die hard – even when people want to change their behaviour, it is not easy for them.

- **People want to do the 'right' thing**. There are cases where money is de-motivating as it undermines people's intrinsic motivation – for example, you would quickly stop inviting friends to dinner if they insisted on paying you.

- **People's self-expectations influence how they behave**. They want their actions to be in line with their values and their commitments.

- **People are bad at computing when making decisions**. They put undue weight on recent events and too little on far-off ones. They cannot calculate probabilities well and worry too much about unlikely events. Finally they are strongly influenced by how the problem or information is presented to them.

- **People need to feel involved in order to make a change**. Just giving people the incentives and information is not necessarily enough.

Many people can be forgiven for looking at this and saying 'I wouldn't fall for any of those traps'. But the reality is that many of us do fall victim to cognitive biases thanks to heuristics – because we are not aware we are taking a short cut at the time. These examples show people can be misguided into making the wrong decisions which may hurt them financially and multiplied across an economy can be quite costly.

Anchoring

People are often influenced by the first number that they see when faced with a choice or a puzzle. For instance if the wine listed at the top of the *carte des vins* in a restaurant or most prominently displayed in an off-licence is £39.99 then the customer will feel they have a bargain if they choose the next one they see at £29.99 even if they could have found one at £14.99 if they had continued to look. Similarly many diners do not want to appear 'cheap' and so will ignore the house wine at £9.99 and plump for the second cheapest even if that is priced at £19.99 and actually not as good value as the house.

Hot-hand fallacy

This focuses on the belief that someone who has had a run of successes at a particular task such as playing football or trading currencies has a higher chance of repeating that success as a result. For example, the fact that a stockbroker's purchases rise in value each day may be nothing to do with their skill but be due to other outside factors. This relates to the **gambler's fallacy** that explains why people believe that a coin which has landed on tails nine times in a row has a greater chance of landing on heads on the tenth toss (the chance is 50:50 every toss – unless the coin is weighted). At the Monte Carlo casino in the summer of 1913, the ball famously fell on black 26 times in a row. Gamblers lost millions of francs by betting that at some point it would be followed by a run of reds. The financial danger in both cases is that investors see a pattern in a random series that does not exist.

Loss aversion

People clearly enjoy making a profit on an investment and dislike losing money when a financial transaction turns sour. But research by Kahneman and Tversky has suggested that the pain associated with a financial loss is two to three times greater than the pleasure associated with an equivalent gain. In an experiment they gave people a choice between an 85% chance to lose $1,000 (with a 15% chance to lose nothing) and a sure loss of $800. A large majority of people expressed a preference for the gamble over the sure loss. People are often unwilling to sell their home for less than they paid for it even if it is clear that prices are likely to fall further.

Herd effect

Behavioural economics can explain stock market booms by pointing to the herd effect, in which people will follow people they know and respect in buying houses or shares in the belief that those people know something that they themselves do not, and that past performance is a guide to the future. Equally, people may not save enough for their retirement because they find it hard to calculate the value of the money they spend now relative to the value it will create over time if left in a savings account.

Nudge, nudge

Understanding the reasons why people behave irrationally can help politicians design policies in a way that encourages positive behaviour. It has been called 'libertarian paternalism' as it encourages people to make the 'right decision' by influencing their freely made decisions. It is also called 'nudge' economics after Thaler's book. The idea was put into practice in the UK by Prime Minister David Cameron who set up the Behavioural Insights Team in the Cabinet Office, which is better known as the 'nudge unit'. It says it has notched up a number of successes that have saved the government money by, for example, altering the wording on tax forms, to changing what happens when you walk into a job centre and giving consumers data on their weekly food shopping.

brilliant example

One example of the practical purpose of behavioural economics is the use of social norms. In a trial the unit sent letters to 140,000 late UK taxpayers. Some received a standard letter and others received one with an added message which mentioned the fact that most people in the recipient's local area, or postcode, had already paid. There was a 15 percentage point difference in the response rate from the traditional letter and the localised one, with more responses from the localised letter. Her Majesty's Revenue and Customs estimated that this effect, if rolled out and repeated across the country, could speed up £160 million of tax debts to the Exchequer over the six-week period of the trial. This would free up resources capable of generating £30 million of extra revenue annually.

Another area where nudge economics may play a role is in pensions savings. A study in the United States in 2001 found that only a third (37%) of people signed up to a commitment to pay into a 401(k) pension plan when they had to sign up for it. However, when joining was made the default – so the workers had to actively sign out – the participation rate rose to 86%. In the UK, the National Employment Savings Trust (NEST) pension scheme being rolled out from late 2012 uses a similar technique. Anyone over 22 who earns enough to pay income tax and who does not have an existing pension scheme will be automatically enrolled into a NEST-qualifying scheme by their employer. Those who do not want to participate need to opt out.

As well as saving for old age and paying tax, behavioural economists have shown how nudges can influence credit markets, environmental policy, healthcare, organ donation and even marriage. The reason why it is both interesting and in this book is because these techniques use markets rather than laws – even if the effect is what lawmakers wanted. It is certain to change the way that economies run as the theories are developed and refined.

Happiness, oh happiness

One of the problems with traditional macroeconomics is that one of its key measures of success is an increasing size of gross domestic product (GDP) or economic activity. But as we saw in Chapter 2 this can include activities that do us harm either individually, such as smoking, or collectively, such as environmental pollution. It also fails to measure many elements of human life that bring happiness to people, such as love, trust, honesty and charity.

However recent years – and particularly since the onset of the 2007/08 financial crisis – have seen a flurry of activity among economists who are studying what constitutes happiness and making recommendations to governments about how best to increase it. The culmination of this effort was in April last year when three of the world's leading experts in economic happiness published a World Happiness Report that had been commissioned by the United Nations.

The UK's Richard Layard, Jeffrey Sachs of the US and John Helliwell of Canada found that while happier countries do tend to be richer countries, social factors like the strength of social support, the absence of corruption and the degree of personal freedom are much greater contributors to happiness than income. Unemployment causes as much unhappiness as bereavement or separation. At work, job security and good relationships do more for job satisfaction than high pay and convenient hours. Mental health is the biggest single factor affecting happiness in any country. Yet only a quarter of mentally ill people get treatment for their condition in advanced countries and fewer in poorer countries.

> happier countries do tend to be richer countries

They said that higher GDP was a valuable goal but should not be pursued to the sacrifice of economic stability, community cohesion, ethical behaviour and care for the vulnerable or environmental sustainability. They said that policymakers needed to take four steps to improve policy-making: better measurement of happiness; more thorough understanding of happiness; putting happiness at the centre of analysis; and translation of wellbeing research into design and delivery of services.

 brilliant fact

In 1972 the Fourth King of Bhutan, a small landlocked state in south Asia that has the 75th lowest GDP per head, declared Gross National Happiness to be more important than Gross National Product (GNP), and from this time onward, the country oriented its national policy and development plans towards GNH. It has nine pillars: living standards (such as income, assets, housing); health; education; the use of time and time poverty; good governance; ecological resilience; psychological wellbeing (which includes overall happiness); community vitality; and cultural diversity and resilience. The GNH Index is based on a survey of 7,142 people.

In 2008 then French president Nicolas Sarkozy asked a team led by two Nobel economists, Joseph Stiglitz and Amartya Sen, to identify the limits of GDP as an indicator of economic performance and social progress, and look

> the limits of GDP as an indicator of economic performance and social progress

at finding an alternative measure. They called on world leaders to move away from a purely economic concept of GDP, which measures economic production, to well-being and sustainability. That report suggested a shift from production to greater attention to household wealth and an assessment of whether countries were growing sustainably or damaging the environment. It broke wellbeing down into categories similar to the Bhutan measure to include political voice and governance, and social connections and relationships.

The UK government is also working on its own General Well Being (GWB) Index. Potential indicators include health, education, income inequalities and the environment. Launching the plan, David Cameron said while GDP showed whether the economy was growing, it 'didn't show where the growth came from'. The results of the first tranche of detailed subjective data, exploring how happiness and anxiety levels vary according to factors including gender, geographical location and ethnic group, were published in July 2012.

People who took part were asked how happy and how anxious they felt yesterday and generally how satisfied they were with their lives and whether they thought their life worthwhile. On a scale of 1–10 the average rating in the UK for the 'worthwhile' question (7.7) was higher than average ratings for 'life satisfaction' (7.4) and 'happy yesterday' (7.3). For 'anxious yesterday', the UK average was much lower at 3.1 out of 10, where 1 corresponds to 'not at all' anxious, and 10 corresponds to 'completely' anxious. More than one in 10 (10.9%) rated their happiness as less than 5 out of 10 (indicating lower happiness).

One weakness, according to economists, is to confuse wellbeing with happiness. Critics of the current system point to research showing that direct survey measures of happiness do not rise in proportion with GDP per head after a level of around $17,000 a year. The problem is that while GDP can keep rising without limit, measured happiness can only ever reach the top of a simple scale of 1 to 5 or 10 in a survey. In other words, since happiness is not a boundless concept, it is not possible to go beyond total ecstasy.

The research on happiness and economic growth does not show a strong link. Economist Richard Easterlin found that while happiness in poor countries does begin by moving up in step with economic growth, there seemed to be a threshold of $15,000 for annual income per year above which there was no strong link between higher GDP and greater wellbeing. Interestingly he also found that average self-reported happiness in Japan did not increase between 1958 and 1987 although GDP per head increased fivefold over those three decades.

However, some economists criticise the whole exercise as being flawed because it relied on subjective answers to broad questions that can be interpreted in many ways and which rely on people accurately remembering how they felt. Kahneman has carried out experiments that show that how people experience feelings differs from how they remember them later. The Gallup-Healthways Well-Being Index interviews at least 1,000 American adults every day in order to provide a real-time measurement of wellbeing. Kahneman says it shows that being poor makes one miserable, being rich may boost one's life satisfaction but does not improve experienced wellbeing. He says that experienced wellbeing no longer increases beyond a household income of $75,000 a year in areas where housing costs are expensive (the figure is lower where housing costs are less).

Behavioural economists have found that above a certain level people start to worry more about earning more than their friends and neighbours than actually earning more in pure cash terms. One reason is that once people have satisfied basic needs such as food, housing and transport, any extra money they earn is spent on keeping pace with neighbours' wealth – 'keeping up with the Joneses'.

---

brilliant example

An economist called Nick Powdthavee looked at how to calculate the value of intangible assets such as the joy of friendship as well as the value of a pay rise on a scale of one to seven. By designing a happiness equation,

Powdthavee shows in his book, *The Happiness Equation*, that a £1,000 pay rise may deliver an increase of 0.0007 on that scale but seeing friends more often is worth 0.161. This implies swapping a sociable life for an isolated one requires a pay rise of 0.161/0.007 or £230,000 a year. Sadly, as with a lot of economics, the full equation contains too many algebra symbols to print here.

It looks as if GDP will remain the main tool for measuring economic wellbeing for some time. The volume of research that has gone into alternative indicators means that interest in the issue is likely to continue and perhaps at some point a new measure will be brought out to replace or complement GDP. In the meantime it is fair to say that there is a strong relationship between GDP and happiness in poor countries and a weaker one in rich nations. It is interesting to note that Bhutan may have a very low GDP per head but it did happen to be the seventh fastest growing economy in the world in 2012 with annual GDP of 9.9%.

Economics and the environment

Mainstream economics is focused on finding the most efficient way to allocate scarce resources. However, it has been clear since Senator Robert Kennedy criticised the failure of GDP to capture pollution (see Chapter 2) that the pursuit of greater GDP can only come at the expense of the resources available to future generations. This conundrum has encouraged economists to devise new ways of thinking about economics and the environment.

Although economic and environmental objectives are often perceived as being contradictory, it is worth remembering that the natural environment is an important economic asset. It provides natural resources needed to sustain production and consumption. One of the most important is energy. It also provides a place for discharging waste, such as landfill sites and the earth's rivers and oceans. Finally it provides places for people to live and take part in recreational activities and gives people pleasure through the natural landscapes and views.

Environmental economics says that the impact that economic growth has upon the environment is seen by some as a 'market failure'. Economists use this term to describe situations where the self-interested behaviour of individuals does not lead to the most efficient outcome. In 1996 the British economist Nicholas (now Lord) Stern, who has been commissioned by the UK government to analyse the economics of climate change, described the problem as the 'greatest market failure the world has ever seen'.

> the impact that economic growth has upon the environment is seen by some as a 'market failure'

At the heart of the problem is another economic term: externalities. These are benefits or costs that are borne by people who were not part of the transactions. Many of the people who are or will be affected by pollution or climate change were not involved in the activity that led to the pollution by, for example, buying an air ticket. In both cases the price is the result of competition between airlines to set the ticket price at a level that allows them to make a profit after paying for the costs of the plane, fuel, airport slot baggage handling, staff and so on.

But it does not pay for the cost of pollution or for the depletion of natural resources such as the oil reserves needed for aviation fuel or the aluminium. Martin Weitzman, a professor at Harvard University who is an acknowledged expert of environmental economics, has estimated that the use of resources that are not renewable costs the equivalent of about 1% of average consumption each year. In 1999 when he did the research,

1% of world consumption represented an enormous amount of goods and services, being equivalent today to about $250 billion a year. He pointed out that that was more than the entire economic output of 95% of the countries in the world.

There is an attempt to ensure that that the user pays the full environmental costs of their air ticket. British Airways was one of the first airlines to introduce a voluntary carbon offset scheme for its passengers. It uses customer donations, which vary according to whether it is a short-, medium- or long-haul flight, to support energy efficiency and renewable energy projects in the UK.

Economists also talk about the 'tragedy of the commons'. It refers to natural resources that can freely be used by anyone. The theory was developed at a time when herders were able to allow their animals to graze on common land. A herder can add an extra animal but that will mean there will be less grass for the other herders' animals. Over time there is nothing to stop herders adding more and more animals until there is no grass left. In more recent times the fact that the oceans are freely available to all has led to overfishing that has driven some breeds to the edge of extinction.

Pricing the problem

Observant readers – especially those who are frequent flyers – will point out that many airlines give travellers an option to pay an extra charge to offset the emission of greenhouse gases from their flight. Others will note that fishing – at least in the waters off the shores of the European Union – is regulated by quotas that limit how many fish each country can land in their ports.

These examples are two of the ways in which policymakers try to limit the impact of the damage on the shared environment. Quotas put an arbitrary limit on the amount of the natural resource that people can use without facing a legal sanction. An alternative is to make a harmful activity illegal. An example is the UK's Clean Air Act 1956 that was passed in response to the 'great smog' of 1952 and which made it illegal in certain cities to burn fuels that produced smoke. However, any legal control requires the state to monitor, investigate and prosecute.

Economics seeks to make the price that users pay reflect the wider costs. The optional BA charge is one way of doing that but the price is set by the airline and so may or may not reflect the full costs. When BA launched the charge it was calculated according to the distance of the journey. However, BA moved to a system with three fixed prices after finding that customers were less likely to pay the highest charges.

Another option is to create a market mechanism to set a price. The European Union has established the Emissions Trading System (ETS) that gives certain polluting industries allowances to pollute. This provides an incentive for companies to reduce their pollution as that will leave them with unused allowances they can sell to less efficient companies. As of January 2013, the EU ETS covers more than 11,000 factories, power stations and other installations. An alternative is to impose a tax that is intended to cover the cost not contained within the market price.

All these measures can be criticised because it is up to the government to either restrict or outlaw the activity, to set the tax, or to establish the limits and mechanism for the trading system. The success of a ban will depend on how effectively the government can ensure the law is followed. Market mechanisms set by governments can be subject to political interference. Critics of the EU ETS say that certain sectors were given more allowances than they need.

Summary

As a subject economics is constantly evolving. The British economist Diane Coyle says in her book *The Soulful Science* that when she attended her first tutorial in 1978 teaching revolved around a neoclassical orthodoxy that included assumptions such as rational choice, utility maximisation and complete information. While some of these have come under attack, the discipline of economics allows new players and models to be introduced. As Coyle says: 'For all that its practitioners criticise [economists] the other social sciences don't have anything approaching the flexibility and strength of the economic method, nor the capacity of economics models to be honed and tested empirically.'

 brilliant recap

- Key assumptions behind neoclassical economics such as the rational agents have come under attack.

- Behavioural economics combines economics and psychology to explain why people make irrational decisions.

- Critics of GDP as the main economic measure want government to measure wellbeing and happiness.

- Concerns over climate change have encouraged new schools of thought.

Brilliant glossary

APR Annual percentage rate. The rate of interest on a loan that includes compound interest and fees and charges.

appreciation When one currency rises in value against another. This makes exports pricier to outsiders but imports cheaper. Opposite of **depreciation**.

asset A thing that belongs to a person or a firm and which has value.

austerity Policies designed to reduce a government **deficit**, most usually tax rises or spending cuts.

bailout Where creditors, often including a government, put together a rescue of a bank or company that is close to bankruptcy.

balance of payments The difference between the money coming into a country over a year and the amount going out.

barter Where goods and services are exchanged without the use of money.

Basel III A global financial regulatory standard agreed by members of the Basel Committee on Banking Supervision, based in the Swiss city of that name. It covers rules on, among others, **capital** adequacy, stress testing and market **liquidity**.

base rate The rate of **interest** charged by the Bank of England to private banks to lend to them. Also bank rate.

basis point One hundredth of 1%, so that 25 basis points means 0.25% or 25 percentage points.

bear market Conditions where asset prices are typically falling and investors are pessimistic.

beggar-my-neighbour Policies aimed at protecting a country's export industry that harm other countries' interests.

behavioural economics A branch of economics that uses psychology to look at the social, cognitive and emotional factors that affect economic decisions.

bond A financial contract that obliges a borrower to repay a loan at a certain time and to make a fixed regular interest payment.

Bretton Woods A town in New Hampshire, US, where the Allies in the Second World War agreed to establish the **International Monetary Fund** and the International Bank for Reconstruction and Development (later the **World Bank**).

BRICS An acronym coined by Goldman Sachs to represent the emerging economies of Brazil, Russia, India and China (and later South Africa).

budget A forecast by a household, firm or government for the amount of money it expects to receive and the amount it intends to spend over a period, usually a year.

bull market Conditions where asset prices are typically rising and investors are optimistic.

capital A stock of wealth held by a company in the form of assets, property and finished goods. Also used to represent financial assets.

capital flight A situation where investors move money quickly out of a country in which they have lost confidence and seek **safe havens**.

capital gains tax A tax levied on a rise in the value of certain assets.

CDO Collateralised debt obligation. A financial product that packages up a mix of bonds and debt instruments into a new asset that is then sold on.

Chicago school A school of economic thought which believes that personal self-interest guides economics decision. Its main advocate was Milton **Friedman**.

classical economics The dominant school of economics for much of the 18th and 19th centuries. It says that the pursuit of self-interest would produce the greatest possible economic benefits for society as a whole through the operation of the **invisible hand**. Founding thinkers included Adam **Smith** and David **Ricardo**.

classical unemployment **Unemployment** that results from wages being too high.

commodities Tangible goods that are the result of a process of production and which are broadly homogeneous whoever makes them. Colloquially it refers to raw materials such as oil, agricultural goods and metals.

comparative advantage A theory of **trade** that identifies activity in which a country is most efficient.

CPI Consumer price index. The index of inflation used by most western policymakers to set interest rates and certain price rises.

creative destruction A theory by economist Joseph **Schumpeter** that **innovation** would create profits for efficient companies at the expense of underperforming ones.

credit crunch Where banks simultaneously refuse to lend because of a fear of borrowers' inability to repay.

credit rating An assessment by a credit rating agency on the likelihood that a borrower will repay its debt. It runs on a scale of AAA to D where BBB – or higher – are seen as 'investment' grade and below are known as 'high yield' or 'junk'.

crowding out The idea that government spending discourages private sector spending either by using up available resources, such as labour, or raising the prices of inputs.

debt The amount of money owed by an individual, firm or government.

deficit The amount by which spending exceeds income over a year.

deflation An average fall in the price of goods and services, usually measured over a year.

demand The amount of a good or service that a consumer – individual, firm or government – is willing and able to buy.

depreciation When one currency falls in value against another. This makes exports cheaper to outsiders but imports more expensive. Opposite of **appreciation**.

depression An extended period of falling output and rising unemployment; a more prolonged and severe version of a **recession**.

derivative A financial instrument whose value is derived from the change in price of other assets. They include options that can be exercised in the future and which are used for **hedging**.

developed country An economy that has gone through the process of industrialisation and which is based on high-value manufacturing and services. Also known as 'advanced', 'industrialised' or 'rich' countries which tend to have sophisticated financial systems.

developing country An economy that has not industrialised and is broadly dependent on agriculture.

direct taxes Taxes that are levied on income and gains in wealth. See also **indirect taxes**.

disinflation A slowdown in the rate of inflation – i.e. prices are rising on average at a slower rate.

easing Adjective often applied to **fiscal policy, monetary policy** or **money** that denotes policies aimed at expanding the economy. Antonym of **tight**.

emerging economy Country that is going through a period of rapid economic growth and industrialisation.

employment Where someone does work for a firm in exchange for pay.

EMU Economic and monetary union in Europe. The agreements that allowed the creation of the euro currency.

exchange rate The price at which the currency of one country can be bought using another country's currency.

expectations In economics, the view of economic agents of what will happen in terms of economic indicators and asset prices.

exports Sales of goods and services by firms in one country to customers in other countries.

fiscal policy Policies by governments that increase or reduce either expenditure or taxation, in order to achieve a specific goal or to stimulate or curb economic **growth**.

frictional Of unemployment, the condition where people are out of work because they are in between jobs.

Friedman, Milton American economist best known for his theories of monetarism; he won the Nobel prize for economics in 1976. A key figure in the **Chicago school**.

full employment A condition where everyone who wants a job and is willing to work has one.

fundamentals In economics, the set of factors that economists see as influencing an economy's future performance.

G7, G8, G20, G24 Groupings of countries with similar economic profiles. They have no direct power but influence economic debate through their communiqués.

GDP Gross domestic product. A measure of a country's output calculated by adding consumption, investment, government spending and exports after subtracting imports.

globalisation The trend towards greater interdependency and integration between workers, firms and governments in different countries by reducing barriers to trade. Generally seen as spreading free-market liberal economic policies.

growth The rate at which a country's economic output increases over a period of time, usually a year.

Hayek, Friedrich Austrian economist (1899–1992) who was a key member of the **Chicago school** and an intellectual opponent of John Maynard **Keynes**. Won the Nobel prize for economics in 1974.

hedge A financial contract whose purpose is to protect the buyer from economic loss depending on a future event taking place, such as the fall in price of an asset or commodity or a move in an exchange rate.

hyperinflation A situation where **inflation** is high and accelerating and appears out of control.

hysteresis A lag between a change in the economy and its impact. Commonly used in terms of **unemployment** where joblessness persists even after the economy has recovered from the downturn that caused the unemployment.

IMF International Monetary Fund. An international financial institution that monitors countries' economies and intervenes with loans in cases of financial crisis.

imports Purchases of goods and services by firms in one country to customers in other countries.

index-linked Where a payment is linked to rises in **inflation**.

indirect tax **Taxes** that are levied on income or profits. Examples include VAT on the purchase of goods and services generally and specific levies such as duties on fuel and on airline tickets.

industrialisation The process during which a **developing country** moves from dependence on agriculture towards manufacturing or services industries.

inflation A persistent increase in the average price of a basket of goods and services.

innovation Developing new goods and services that can be sold in the market – or designing new methods of production.

input One of the four factors that go into production (land, machinery, **labour** and **capital**).

interest rate The cost of borrowing money or other assets expressed as a percentage of the amount borrowed. Also used to refer to central banks' **base rate**.

investment The acquisition of an asset for the purpose of generation of future wealth.

invisible hand The phrase coined by economist Adam **Smith** to describe how the economy works most efficiency if consumers and firms are allowed to follow their own self-interest to seek profit.

Juglar cycle A business cycle of 7–11 years that is driven by flows in investments in fixed capital by companies.

Keynes, John Maynard British economist (1883–1946) whose theories on economics arose out of the Great

Depression and which are seen as the foundation of macroeconomics.

Keynesian economics The belief that governments need to use fiscal policy to achieve full employment in a stagnating economy by borrowing money to invest.

Kondratieff wave A business cycle of 45–60 years, also known as a super-cycle.

labour The input into production made up of people willing and able to work.

LIBOR London interbank offered rate. The rate at which banks in London lend money to each other for the short term in a particular currency.

liquidity A situation of having cash or assets that can be instantly converted into cash.

liquidity trap A situation where **monetary policy** becomes impotent, as policymakers are unable to stimulate the economy by lowering rates further as consumers and firms prefer to save.

Marx, Karl German economist (1818–83) who used classical economics to show how capitalism would sow the seeds of its own destruction. He said competition would drive prices down to levels at which low wages would lead to mass discontent. His thinking was used by communist governments as the basis for their policies.

monetary policy The tools by which a central bank controls the **money supply** in order to manage demand and control inflation. These include changing the short term **interest rate** and **quantitative easing**.

money Tool to buy goods and service that has three attributes: a medium of exchange; a unit of account; a store of value.

money supply The amount of money that exists in an economy. It is calculated in various ways, notably narrow money (cash and instant access bank accounts) and broad money (cash, current account deposits, savings deposits and time-restricted deposits).

multiplier The way that an increase in spending, such as by governments, leads to a much higher increase in income.

NAIRU Non-accelerating inflation rate of unemployment. The rate of **unemployment** at which inflation remains stable.

negative equity Where the value of the property is less than the size of the mortgage debt against it.

nominal The value or price of anything expressed in the actual money of the day not taking inflation into account (see **real terms**).

OECD The Organisation for Economic Co-operation and Development. An association of, and think tank for around 30 industrialised economies.

OPEC The Organisation of Petroleum Exporting Countries. A cartel of the leading oil producers that can exert huge influence over the market price of crude oil. Blamed for 1979s **recession**.

opportunity cost The cost of the alternative that must be foregone as the result of a decision to allocate resources on one activity.

overheating When economic activity rises to such a level that it creates inflation.

permanent income hypothesis Theorem devised by Milton **Friedman** which says that consumers should spread their spending over their lifetime and not spend one-off windfalls.

Phillips curve A graph showing a trade-off between inflation and unemployment that appeared to hold true during the

1950s and 1960s but the relationship broke down in the 1970s and 1980s when it was superseded by the **NAIRU**.

PPP Purchasing power parity. An exchange rate based on the amount of one currency needed to purchase a basket of goods and services relative to others.

productivity The amount of output by worker or per hour of work.

progressive A tax system in which the percentage paid increases as income rises.

protectionism Policies aimed at protecting a country's domestic industry buy putting up tariff barriers to others' imports. See also **beggar-thy-neighbour**.

quantitative easing Central banks **easing monetary policy** by increasing the **money supply** and using the new money to buy government bonds or other categories of assets in order to lower interest rates.

quantity theory of money A key theory of monetarism that quantity of money in the economy determines the level of prices.

ratings See **credit rating**.

rational expectations The idea that people can on average make an assessment of how the economy will behave based on a rational interpretation of all the information available to them and act accordingly.

real terms A measure of value or inflation that takes account of inflation. Opposite of **nominal**.

recession A period when the size of an economy shrinks. Many countries use a definition of two consecutive quarters of falling **GDP**.

Ricardian equivalence The idea that government deficits used to fund efforts to stimulate the economy will not work because consumers will foresee the **tax** rises needed to pay for them.

Ricardo, David English economist (1772–1823) who developed the theories of **comparative advantage** and what is now known as **Ricardian equivalance**.

RPI Retail price index. An official UK measure of inflation that was introduced in 1947 but which has been generally superseded by **CPI**.

safe haven/harbour An economy that financial investors see as the best option for their money in times of volatility.

savings Income that is not spent. Often used to refer to money put into savings accounts, pensions and shares.

scarcity One of the key concepts that underlies micro- and macroeconomics. It is the idea that resources are finite and, given that demand is infinite, there needs to be a system for allocating those scarce resources.

Schumpeter, Joseph Austrian economist (1883–1950) best known for his theory of **creative destruction**.

shock A negative and unforeseeable event that affects a country's economy.

Smith, Adam Scottish economist (1723–90) best known for his book *The Wealth of Nations* and for establishing the school of **classical economics**. Theories include the **invisible hand** and the division of labour.

speculation A very short-term form of investment where investors deploy their **capital** in pursuit of a quick profit by buying and selling assets in quick succession.

spread The gap between the price or interest rate on two different financial products. In financial trading it is the gap between the prices at which a dealer will buy and sell the same asset.

stickiness The idea that prices and wages do not respond quickly to changes in economic **demand**. This can be because firms have long-term contracts and because of the inconvenience and cost of changing prices. A key element of the theories of John Maynard **Keynes**.

structural unemployment Long-term **unemployment** that does not improve in line with the economic cycle. It is a result of a structural change in the economy which means workers no longer have relevant skills.

supply The quantity of a good or service that is available at a certain price. It is one of the primary driving forces of market economics along with **demand**.

supply-side reforms Measures aimed at making the economy work more efficiently rather than trying to stimulate **demand**. They include measures such as deregulation, privatisation and greater competition.

tariff A **tax** imposed by a government on goods imported from other countries to make them more expensive than domestically produced alternatives.

tax Compulsory payments by people, firms and institutions to the government. They are sub-divided between **direct taxes** on income and wealth and **indirect taxes** levied on purchases of goods, services and assets.

tight Description of economic policies that aim to restrict the rate of economic **growth** and **inflation**.

trade Sales and purchases of goods and services between people, firms and governments in different countries. It is made up of **exports** and **imports**.

tragedy of the commons The depletion of common resources that are not owned by any one user but can be used without limit by all.

transmission mechanism The way that changes in **interest rates** affect changes in economic **growth** and **inflation**.

unemployment The number of people between specific ages (traditionally 16–64) who are without work but who are seeking a job and able to work.

velocity of circulation The speed at which money moves through the economy or the number of times the same sum of money changes hands. A key component of **monetarist** theories.

voluntary unemployment People who are able to work but choose not to either because wages are too low or because they prefer to live on government benefits.

wages Money paid to a worker for work done.

wealth The value of assets held by a household, firm or government.

windfall Unexpected and usually large amount of extra income. The **permanent income hypothesis** says that recipients will spend the money over the course of their lives rather than in one go.

World Bank International financial institution with its origins in the **Bretton Woods** agreement of 1944. It provides financial and technical assistance to developing countries around the world.

World Trade Organisation An international forum for governments to negotiate trade agreements and a place for them to settle trade disputes.

yield The rate of return to an investor from buying a bond that is implied by the bond's current market price. The yield moves in an opposite direction from its price. The difference in the yield of one bond compared with another's is known as the **spread**.

yield curve A graph that shows how yields on bonds change according to the timespan of the bond. The yield usually increases as the duration rises to take account of the **opportunity cost** to investors by tying up their **money** for longer.

Useful websites

This book does not include a bibliography, as there are so many books that look at each of the concepts in this *'Brilliant'* introductory book that it would not be possible to list them all. Anyone interested in one area, whether growth, inflation or behavioural economics for example, can easily find useful reference works.

However there are many websites, run by institutions or individual economists, that provide a useful resource to the latest thinking on economics and act as pointers to new research or writing for those interested. They also have the benefit of offering readers the chance to dip in and out. Here is a select number with a brief description of what to expect.

http://www.tutor2u.net/blog/index.php/economics/

This is an online community of teachers and students. Aimed primarily at GCSE and A level students of economics and business studies, it contains explanations and videos about core concepts, entries based on recent news events and discussions between members.

http://timharford.com/articles/undercovereconomist/

Tim Harford is a senior columnist for the *Financial Times*. His long-running column, 'The Undercover Economist', reveals the economic ideas behind everyday experiences, while a new column, 'Since You Asked', offers a sceptical look at the news of the week. As a broadcaster, Tim has presented television and radio series for the BBC. His books include *The Undercover Economist*.

http://www.enlightenmenteconomics.com/blog/

This a key resource for following the latest books on economics published on both sides of the Atlantic. Diane Coyle is a writer and Harvard PhD who runs the consultancy Enlightenment Economics. Her most recent book is *The Economics of Enough*.

http://stumblingandmumbling.typepad.com/

A blog written by Chris Dillow, an economics writer at the *Investors Chronicle* magazine. He blogs on investment-related economics issues. He is the author of *New Labour and the End of Politics*.

http://mainlymacro.blogspot.co.uk/

This is a blog on macroeconomic issues written for both economists and non-economists by Simon Wren-Lewis, an economics professor at Oxford University, and a fellow of Merton College.

http://www.bbc.co.uk/news/correspondents/stephanieflanders/

The blog is written by Stephanie Flanders, the Economics Editor of the BBC and gives her take on major breaking economics news stories. Before working at the BBC, she was a reporter at the *New York Times*; a speech writer and senior adviser to the US Treasury Secretary; a *Financial Times* leader-writer and columnist; and an economist at the Institute for Fiscal Studies.

http://www.ezonomics.com/

eZonomics is about money and people's lives. It combines ideas around financial education, personal finance and behavioural economics to produce regular and practical information about the way people manage their money – and how this can affect their lives. It is funded by ING and produced in ING's global economics department.

http://www.freakonomics.com/

This website arose out of the huge success of the book *Freakonomics* by economics professor Steven Levitt and journalist and author Stephen Dubner, which has sold more than 4 million copies in 35 languages. The website includes blogs by both authors and links to their lectures.

http://www.learnliberty.org/category/economics

This is a US-based website that features videos recorded by academic economics commentators. It takes broadly a free-market stand, highlighting thinkers such as Adam Smith and more recent scholars such as Friedrich Hayek and Milton Friedman. It includes videos of Professor Tyler Cowen, who also writes for the blog http://marginalrevolution.com/, which explain core economic principles.

http://economics.about.com/

This is a very busy US-oriented website that has articles on questions such as 'What is Economics?' and 'What is Macroeconomics?' Like tutor2u it also uses recent news events to explain economic concepts.

And finally...

http://econstories.tv/2011/04/28/fight-of-the-century-music-video/ and http://econstories.tv/2010/06/22/fear-the-boom-and-bust/

For readers who were interested in the rap videos explaining the classical and Keynesian responses to the 2008/09 financial crisis in the US.

References and further reading

This is a list of major institutions and organisations that produce regular research and information and which anyone interested in learning more about economics should look at on a regular basis. There are many other highly reputable institutions but these are the ones that tend to be most prolific.

INSTITUTE FOR FISCAL STUDIES

www.ifs.org.uk

The IFS is a UK economics think tank. It publishes research in a wide area of issues arising out of tax and spending decisions. In particular it produces an annual report, known as the Green Budget, in January, which gives detailed analysis of what to expect in the Budget.

NATIONAL INSTITUTE OF ECONOMIC AND SOCIAL RESEARCH

www.niesr.ac.uk

Britain's longest established independent economic research institute with over 60 years' experience. It falls into three distinct fields: economic modelling and macro analysis; education, training and employment; the international economy. It produces monthly estimates of UK GDP and detailed quarterly outlooks for the global economy.

THE NATIONAL BUREAU OF ECONOMIC RESEARCH

www.nber.org

Based in the US and similar to the NIESR, it undertakes and disseminates unbiased economic research among public policy-makers, business professionals and the academic community. Its foci are: developing new statistical measurements, estimating quantitative models of economic behaviour, assessing the economic effects of public policies and projecting the effects of alternative policy proposals.

VOX

www.voxeu.org

This is a portal for research-based policy analysis and commentary by leading scholars, usually rewritten for a more lay audience. Its readership includes economists in governments, international organisations, academia and the private sector as well as journalists specialising in economics, finance and business.

ECONOMIC AND SOCIAL RESEARCH COUNCIL

www.esrc.ac.uk

The UK's largest organisation for funding research on economic and social issues. It supports independent, high quality research, which has an impact on business, the public sector and the third sector. It produces regular press releases, features, evidence briefings and videos based on the research it has sponsored.

INTERNATIONAL MONETARY FUND

www.imf.org

This giant international financial institution produces daily updates on speeches by its senior figures, reports on countries and issues and provides links to its quarterly economic forecasts. It also has a country index that allows students and economists to get detailed information.

CENTER FOR GLOBAL DEVELOPMENT

www.cgdev.org

There are many good organisations looking at development economics but this is probably the best place to start. The CGD aims to combine world-class research with policy analysis and innovative communications to turn ideas into action. It looks at a range of issues under the development umbrella and produces regular publications and podcasts.

Index

Note: Entries in bold also appear in the Glossary